dim sum

dim sum

Editor: Lydia Leong
Designer: Lock Hong Liang
Series Designer: Bernard Go Kwang Meng

Copyright © 2008 Marshall Cavendish International (Asia) Private Limited
Reprinted 2009

Published by Marshall Cavendish Cuisine
An imprint of Marshall Cavendish International
1 New Industrial Road, Singapore 536196

All rights reserved

No part of this publication may be reproduced, stored in a retrieval system or transmitted, in any form or by any means, electronic, mechanical, photocopying, recording or otherwise, without the prior permission of the copyright owner. Request for permission should be addressed to the Publisher, Marshall Cavendish International (Asia) Private Limited, 1 New Industrial Road, Singapore 536196. Tel: (65) 6213 9300, Fax: (65) 6285 4871. E-mail: te@sg.marshallcavendish.com

Limits of Liability/Disclaimer of Warranty: The Author and Publisher of this book have used their best efforts in preparing this book. The Publisher makes no representation or warranties with respect to the contents of this book and is not responsible for the outcome of any recipe in this book. While the Publisher has reviewed each recipe carefully, the reader may not always achieve the results desired due to variations in ingredients, cooking temperatures and individual cooking abilities. The Publisher shall in no event be liable for any loss of profit or any other commercial damage, including but not limited to special, incidental, consequential, or other damages.

Other Marshall Cavendish Offices:
Marshall Cavendish Ltd. 5th Floor, 32-38 Saffron Hill, London EC1N 8FH, UK • Marshall Cavendish Corporation. 99 White Plains Road, Tarrytown NY 10591-9001, USA • Marshall Cavendish International (Thailand) Co Ltd. 253 Asoke, 12th Flr, Sukhumvit 21 Road, Klongtoey Nua, Wattana, Bangkok 10110, Thailand • Marshall Cavendish (Malaysia) Sdn Bhd, Times Subang, Lot 46, Subang Hi-Tech Industrial Park, Batu Tiga, 40000 Shah Alam, Selangor Darul Ehsan, Malaysia

Marshall Cavendish is a trademark of Times Publishing Limited

National Library Board Singapore Cataloguing in Publication Data

Dim sum. - Singapore : Marshall Cavendish Cuisine, c2008.
p. cm. - (Mini cookbooks)
ISBN-13 : 978-981-261-541-1
ISBN-10 : 981-261-541-5

1. Dim sum. 2. Cookery, Chinese. 3. Desserts. I. Series: Mini cookbooks

TX724.5.C5
641.5951 -- dc22   OCN179734785

Printed in Singapore by Saik Wah Press Pte Ltd

spring onion pancakes 10
flower bloom dumplings 12
crispy seaweed rolls 14
spring onion patties 17
cabbage and bean curd patties 18
steamed minced meat dumplings 21
golden pouches 22
fried chive knots 25
aubergine folders 26
mixed vegetable patties 28
lotus root salad 31
shanghai pancakes 32
sweet potatoes in syrup 35

contents

toffee apple fritters 36
steamed milk egg 39
lotus root agar-agar 40
banana gelatine 43
sweet-scented lychees 44
sweet dumplings 47
glutinous rice with fruit 48
stir-fried egg yolks 51
sweet yam paste (au nee) 52
white fungus dessert 55
lily bulb petals with lotus seeds 56

winter melon delight 59
lotus root with red dates 60
longan dessert with gingko nuts 63
peanut crème 64
gingko nut and water chestnut dessert 67
mung bean soup 68
mung bean dessert 71
fu chok tong shui 72
chestnut soup with osmanthus blossoms 75
barley soup 76
white fungus and wolfberry soup 79
weights and measures 80

dim sum

spring onion pancakes Makes 4

Fragrant with the aroma of spring onions, these crisp Chinese pancakes can be enjoyed on their own or as an accompaniment to rice porridge.

INGREDIENTS

Spring onions (scallions)	6, finely sliced
Salt	1 tsp
Cooking oil	4 Tbsp

SCALDED DOUGH

Plain (all-purpose) flour	300 g (11 oz)
Boiling water	300 ml (10 fl oz / 1$1/4$ cups)

METHOD

- Prepare scalded dough. Sift flour into a mixing bowl. Add boiling water gradually while stirring continuously to mix well. Cover bowl with a damp cloth and let stand for about 10 minutes.

- Knead mixture into a rough dough. Add more flour or water, if necessary. Dough should feel damp but not wet. Cover with a damp cloth and let stand for another 20 minutes.

- Knead dough vigorously by pushing and pulling it apart. Finish off by kneading dough for about 15–20 minutes until dough is smooth.

- Divide dough into 4 and roll each piece to 0.5-cm ($1/4$-in) thickness. Brush with a little oil, then sprinkle with spring onions and salt. Roll dough into a ball, then flatten into a round about 12-cm (5-in) in diameter.

- Heat oil in a pan and fry pancakes over medium heat until golden brown on both sides. Drain well and serve hot.

flower bloom dumplings Makes 12

The ingredients used for the topping can be varied as desired. Choose vegetables with vibrant colours for an attractive presentation.

INGREDIENTS

Chinese cabbage	150 g (5$^1/_3$ oz), finely minced
Salt	$^1/_2$ Tbsp
Firm bean curd	55 g (2 oz), cut into small cubes
Dried Chinese mushrooms	3, soaked to soften, stems discarded and finely minced
Water chestnuts	2, peeled and finely minced
Ginger	2.5-cm (1-in) knob, peeled and finely minced
Wonton wrappers	12 sheets
Corn flour (cornstarch)	1 Tbsp, mixed with 2 Tbsp water

SEASONING

Sesame oil	1 tsp
Salt	$^1/_4$ tsp
Ground white pepper	$^1/_4$ tsp

TOPPING

Carrot	55 g (2 oz), peeled and chopped
Canned bamboo shoot	55 g (2 oz), chopped
Celery	55 g (2 oz), chopped
Dried Chinese mushrooms	3, soaked to soften, stems discarded and chopped

METHOD

- Sprinkle Chinese cabbage with salt and let stand for 5 minutes. Rinse cabbage, then wrap in a tea towel and squeeze out all excess moisture. Mix with bean curd, mushrooms, water chestnuts, ginger and seasoning to make filling. Divide into 12 equal portions.
- Spoon 1 portion of filling onto the centre of a wonton wrapper. Dab thumb and forefinger of both hands with corn flour mixture and pinch all 4 corners of wonton skin together to meet in the centre of each square wrapper to form 4 'pockets'. Open 'pockets' up and top each one with a different topping ingredient.
- Place dumplings on a greased steaming plate. Cover and steam over boiling water for 10 minutes. Serve hot.

crispy seaweed rolls Serves 4

Lightly frying the seaweed rolls gives them a wonderful crisp texture.

INGREDIENTS

Carrot	1, peeled and cut into long, thin strips
Cucumber	1/2, peeled and cut into long, thin strips
Canned bamboo shoot	55 g (2 oz), drained and cut into long, thin strips
Wood ear fungus	55 g (2 oz), soaked to soften and finely sliced
Salt	1/2 tsp
Nori (seaweed)	3 sheets
Plain (all-purpose) flour	2 Tbsp, mixed with 1 1/2 Tbsp water
Cooking oil	2 Tbsp

DIP

Light soy sauce	3 Tbsp
Water	3 Tbsp
Corn flour (cornstarch)	2 tsp
Chilli powder	1/2 tsp

METHOD

- Place carrot, cucumber, bamboo shoot and wood ear fungus in a colander and sprinkle with salt.

- Lay nori sheets on a flat working surface and arrange an equal portion of vegetables, bamboo shoot and wood ear fungus on each sheet. Roll up and seal ends with flour paste.

- Prepare dip. Combine dip ingredients in a small saucepan. Stir well and bring to the boil. Remove from heat and set aside to cool.

- Heat oil in a frying pan and pan-fry seaweed rolls over medium heat for 5 minutes, turning them constantly.

- Remove and slice thickly. Serve with dip on the side.

spring onion patties Makes 4

With a crisp shell and a chewy texture inside, these spring onion patties can also be enjoyed with minced meat. Replace one-third of the spring onion and bean curd mixture with minced meat and stir-fry to cook the meat lightly before placing in the scalded dough.

INGREDIENTS

Spring onions (scallions)	280 g (10 oz), minced
Yellow pressed bean curd	220 g (8 oz), mashed
Cooking oil	4 Tbsp
Scalded dough (page 10)	1 quantity

SEASONING

Salt	2 tsp
Ground white pepper	$1/2$ tsp
Sesame oil	1 tsp

METHOD

- Place spring onions, bean curd and seasoning in a large bowl and mix well. Set aside to use as filling for patties.
- Divide scalded dough into 4 pieces. Roll each piece into a ball, then roll out into a round about 16-cm (6$1/2$-in) in diameter.
- Divide filling into 4 portions. Spoon a portion onto each dough round. Fold dough over to get a semi-circle and enclose mixture. Press edges together and seal with some water.
- Heat oil and pan-fry spring onion patties slowly for 10–15 minutes on each side, until golden brown. Drain well and serve hot.

cabbage and bean curd patties Makes 8

These cabbage and bean curd patties can be enjoyed on their own or dipped into chilli sauce.

INGREDIENTS

Chinese cabbage	450 g (1 lb)
Salt	2 tsp
Soft bean curd	300 g (11 oz), drained and mashed
Dried Chinese mushrooms	5, soaked to soften, stems discarded and minced
Scalded dough (page 10)	1 quantity
Cooking oil	90 ml (3 fl oz / 6 Tbsp)

SEASONING

Light soy sauce	1/2 Tbsp
Sugar	1/2 Tbsp
Ground white pepper	1 tsp
Corn flour (cornstarch)	1 Tbsp
Sesame oil	1/2 Tbsp

METHOD

- Rub cabbage with salt and leave for 10 minutes. Wash salt off cabbage and gently squeeze out excess water using hands. Chop finely. Mix mashed bean curd with cabbage, mushrooms and seasoning.

- Knead scalded dough until smooth and glossy. Divide into 8 portions. Roll each portion into a ball, then flatten into rounds about 6-cm (2 1/2-in) in diameter. Spoon 1–2 Tbsp cabbage mixture onto the centre of each round, then enclose. Roll dough into a ball, then flatten using a rolling pin.

- Heat oil and pan-fry patties for about 10 minutes on each side or until lightly golden. Drain well and serve hot.

steamed minced meat dumplings Makes 12

Sichuan vegetable with its salty flavour and crunchy texture adds both taste and texture to this dim sum dish.

INGREDIENTS

Cooking oil	2 Tbsp
Sichuan vegetable	70 g (2 1/2 oz), soaked in water for 30 minutes, drained and minced
Minced meat	150 g (5 1/3 oz), drained and minced
Scalded dough (page 10)	1 quantity, or 12 wonton wrappers

SEASONING

Sugar	1/2 Tbsp
Light soy sauce	1/2 tsp
Ground white pepper	1/2 tsp
Water	4 Tbsp

METHOD

- Heat oil in a wok and stir-fry Sichuan vegetable and minced meat for 2 minutes, breaking meat up. Add seasoning and mix well. Cover and cook for another 2 minutes, then set aside to cool.

- If using scalded dough, knead dough until smooth, then shape into a long roll. Cut into 12 equal sections, then roll each section into a thin round. Alternatively, use round wonton wrappers and omit this step.

- Spoon 2 tsp Sichuan vegetable and meat mixture onto the centre of each dough round or wonton wrapper. Fold over into semi-circles and pinch the edges of the dough around filling to seal.

- Line a steamer with a sheet of damp muslin, then arrange dumplings on top. Cover and steam over rapidly boiling water for 8–10 minutes. Serve immediately.

golden pouches Makes 10

These attractive little deep-fried pouches can also be served as finger food. Serve with a sweet chilli sauce for dipping, if desired.

INGREDIENTS

Cooking oil	4 Tbsp + more for deep-frying
Garlic	4 cloves, peeled and finely chopped
Soft bean curd	200 g (7 oz), finely diced
Water chestnuts	6, peeled and minced
Carrots	200 g (7 oz), peeled and minced
Dried Chinese mushrooms	6, soaked to soften, stems discarded and finely sliced
Glass noodles	55 g (2 oz), soaked in hot water to soften and drained
Spring onions (scallions)	2, finely chopped + 10, blanched for 2 minutes
Corn flour (cornstarch)	1 tsp, mixed with 1 Tbsp water
Spring roll wrappers	10, each 10-cm (4-in) square

SEASONING

Oyster sauce	2 Tbsp
Light soy sauce	1 tsp
Ground white pepper	1/2 tsp
Sesame oil	1/2 tsp

METHOD

- Heat 4 Tbsp oil in a wok and stir-fry garlic, bean curd, water chestnuts, carrots and mushrooms until lightly fragrant. Mix in seasoning.

- Cut glass noodles into short strands, then add to wok with chopped spring onions. Mix well. Stir in corn flour mixture and cook until sauce is thick. Set aside to cool before using as filling.

- Lay a sheet of spring roll wrapper on a work surface. Spoon 4 tsp filling in the centre, then bring edges of spring roll wrapper together to form a pouch, enclosing filling. Secure pouch with a length of blanched spring onion. Trim pouch top with scissors. Repeat until all ingredients are used up.

- Heat oil for deep-frying and deep-fry pouches until golden brown. Remove with a slotted spoon and drain well. Serve hot.

fried chive knots Makes 12

Flowering chives have a lightly sweet, garlicky flavour and crunchy texture. In Chinese cooking, they are usually stir-fried with other vegetables. Dipped in batter and deep-fried, they make attractive finger foods.

INGREDIENTS

Plain (all-purpose) flour	120 g (4$\frac{1}{2}$ oz)
Salt	$\frac{1}{3}$ tsp
Potato flour	2 Tbsp
Eggs	2, lightly beaten
Water	180 ml (6 fl oz / $\frac{3}{4}$ cup)
Flowering chives	4 bunches
Cooking oil for deep-frying	

DIP

Dark soy sauce	3 Tbsp
Chilli sauce	$\frac{1}{2}$ Tbsp
Sugar	$\frac{1}{2}$ Tbsp
Minced garlic	1 tsp

METHOD

- Mix together plain flour, salt and potato flour in a mixing bowl. Make a well in the centre and add beaten eggs. Stir, adding water gradually, to achieve a smooth batter the consistency of heavy cream. Set aside.

- Discard any withered leaves from chives and wash chives well. Scald a handful of chives in boiling water to soften. Set aside.

- Divide remaining chives into 12 equal bunches. Fold each bunch into bundles about 8-cm (3-in) in length. Bind each bundle together with scalded chives. Coat chive bundles evenly with batter. Heat oil for deep-frying and deep-fry a few chive bundles at a time until golden brown. Drain well.

- Combine ingredients for dip and mix well. Serve on the side with fried chive bundles.

aubergine folders
Makes about 30

A treat for aubergine lovers! Coating the aubergines in batter before cooking helps them retain their shape.

INGREDIENTS

Firm bean curd	220 g (8 oz)
Black moss	5 g ($1/6$ oz), soaked in cold water for 20 minutes and drained
Long purple aubergines (eggplants/brinjals)	4, each about 16-cm ($6^{1}/_{2}$-in) long
Plain (all-purpose) flour	120 g ($4^{1}/_{2}$ oz)
Salt	$1/2$ tsp
Eggs	2, lightly beaten
Cooking oil	1 Tbsp + more for deep-frying
Water	

SEASONING

Salt	$1/2$ tsp
Ground white pepper	$1/2$ tsp
Egg white	1

SAUCE

Oyster sauce	3 Tbsp
Water	$1^{1}/_{2}$ Tbsp
Salt	$1/2$ tsp
Spring onion (scallion)	1, minced
Garlic	2 cloves, peeled and finely minced
Cooking oil	1 Tbsp

METHOD

- Blanch bean curd in boiling water for 3 minutes. Drain and pat dry. Cut off and discard hard outer layer and mash remainder. Mix well with black moss and seasoning. Set aside.

- Wash aubergines and discard ends. Cut into 2-cm (1-in) thick slices, then cut in between each slice, almost through, to make 'folders'. Press $^1/_2$ Tbsp bean curd mixture into each 'folder'.

- Mix flour with salt in a bowl. Make a well in the centre and add beaten eggs and 1 Tbsp oil. Gradually stir flour into eggs, adding sufficient water to make a smooth batter the consistency of heavy cream. Let batter stand for 10 minutes.

- Mix all ingredients for sauce together except oil. Heat oil and add sauce to cook for 2–3 minutes. Set aside.

- Heat cooking oil for deep-frying. Coat aubergine folders with batter and deep-fry for about 4 minutes each, until puffed up and golden brown. Remove with a slotted spoon and drain well. Serve with sauce.

mixed vegetable patties Makes 6

The combination of wood ear fungus, dried lily buds, Sichuan vegetable and water chestnuts all add a delightful crunchy texture to these mixed vegetable patties.

INGREDIENTS

Soft bean curd	300 g (11 oz), drained and mashed
Wood ear fungus	15 g ($\frac{1}{2}$ oz), soaked to soften and finely sliced
Dried lily buds	30 g (1 oz), soaked for 30 minutes, drained and roughly chopped
Sichuan vegetable	45 g ($1\frac{1}{2}$ oz), soaked in water for 20 minutes, drained and finely sliced
Onion	1, small, peeled and minced
Water chestnuts	85 g (3 oz), peeled and minced
Spring onion (scallion)	1, finely minced
Cooking oil	150 ml (5 fl oz / 10 Tbsp)

SEASONING A

Corn flour (cornstarch)	2 Tbsp
Salt	$\frac{1}{2}$ tsp
Ground white pepper	$\frac{1}{2}$ tsp

SEASONING B

Light soy sauce	$1\frac{1}{2}$ Tbsp
Water	3 Tbsp
Sugar	$\frac{1}{2}$ Tbsp

METHOD

- Combine all ingredients except spring onion, oil and seasoning in a bowl and mix well. Add seasoning A and mix well.

- Heat 2 Tbsp oil in a wok and stir-fry mixture for 2 minutes. Remove and set aside. When cool, divide mixture into 6 portions and form into flat, round patties.

- Heat 100 ml (3^1/$_2$ fl oz) oil in a frying pan and cook patties until golden brown on both sides. Dish out.

- Heat remaining oil in a clean frying pan and add seasoning B. Bring to the boil, then pour over patties. Serve immediately.

lotus root salad Serves 6–8

An Asian root vegetable, lotus root is sweet with a crunchy texture. It is commonly boiled in soups, steamed, stir-fried and braised.

INGREDIENTS

Lotus root	300 g (11 oz)
Salt	1 tsp
White vinegar	3 Tbsp
Sugar	4 Tbsp
Spring onion (scallion)	1, chopped (optional)

METHOD

- Wash lotus root well. Peel off skin and cut into thin slices.

- Bring some water to the boil in a pot and blanch lotus root slices briefly. Remove and place into cold water to cool. Drain.

- Place lotus root slices in a large bowl. Add salt, white vinegar and sugar. Toss well.

- Arrange lotus root slices neatly on a serving plate. Garnish with chopped spring onion, if desired. Serve.

shanghai pancakes Serves 4

These crispy pancakes are filled with a thick and sweet red bean paste. Serve at the end of a Chinese meal.

INGREDIENTS

RED BEAN PASTE

Red (adzuki) beans	300 g (11 oz), soaked overnight and drained
Castor (superfine) sugar	200 g (7 oz)
Cooking oil	4 Tbsp

PANCAKE BATTER

Plain (all-purpose) flour	110 g (4 oz)
Salt	1/4 tsp
Egg	1, beaten
Water	250 ml (8 fl oz / 1 cup)
White sesame seeds	2 Tbsp, roasted
Cooking oil	

METHOD

- Prepare red bean paste. Place beans in a pot and cover with water. Bring to the boil and allow mixture to boil for about $2^1/_2$ hours or until beans are soft. Rub beans through a wire strainer using the back of a wooden spoon until only dry pulp is left. Discard pulp. Spoon bean paste into a muslin bag and drip dry before using.

- Heat a clean wok and add bean paste, sugar and oil. Cook for 45 minutes over medium heat, stirring constantly to prevent burning. Cooked bean paste should be smooth and glossy. Set aside.

- Prepare pancakes. Sift flour and salt into a deep mixing bowl. Make a well in the centre, then add beaten egg and half the water. With a wooden spoon, gradually work in flour from all sides. Pour in remaining water and sesame seeds and mix until batter is smooth. Allow batter to stand for about 30 minutes.

- Heat 2 tsp oil small frying pan. Add 2–3 Tbsp pancake batter and cook pancakes for 1 minute on each side until both sides are brown. Transfer to a plate. Repeat process until batter is used up. Add more oil to pan as required.

- Spread pancakes with bean paste and fold in half. Pan-fry each folded pancake on both sides quickly to crisp them. Transfer to a serving plate and serve immediately.

sweet potatoes in syrup Serves 6–8

Choose sweet potatoes that are long and slender and roughly uniform in size for a more attractive presentation. You may also use purple sweet potatoes, if desired.

INGREDIENTS

Light brown sugar	280 g (10 oz)
Water	125 ml (4 fl oz / $^1/_2$ cup)
Cooking oil	3 Tbsp
Sweet potatoes	1 kg (2 lb 3 oz), peeled and cut into 3-cm ($1^1/_2$-in) thick slices

METHOD

- Place brown sugar, water and oil in a pot and heat gently until sugar dissolves.
- Bring to the boil, then add sweet potatoes and return to the boil. Lower heat and simmer gently for 30–35 minutes until sweet potatoes are tender. Serve immediately.

toffee apple fritters Makes 16

Choose sweet red apples with a crisp texture for this dish. Soft apples will not hold their shape as well when deep-fried.

INGREDIENTS

Sugar	225 g (8 oz)
Water	3 Tbsp
Crisp red apples	2, peeled, cored and cut into 8 wedges each
Cooking oil for deep-frying	
Ice water	

BATTER

Plain (all-purpose) flour	125 g (4^1/$_2$ oz)
Baking powder	1^1/$_2$ tsp
Tepid water	150 ml (5 fl oz / 10 Tbsp)

METHOD

- Prepare batter. Sift flour and baking powder into a mixing bowl. Make a well in the centre, then add tepid water gradually and stir to incorporate flour. Mix well to form a smooth batter.

- Place sugar and water in a saucepan and bring to a slow boil, stirring. Continue stirring until sugar syrup has achieved the consistency of thick honey. Remove from heat and leave in pan.

- Heat oil in a wok. Coat apple wedges with batter and deep-fry for 2–3 minutes in batches. Remove with a slotted spoon. Drain and keep warm.

- When apple fritters are ready, reheat sugar syrup in pan until very lightly caramelised. Coat apple fritters thoroughly in caramelised sugar and dip immediately into ice water to cool and set.

- Drain well and serve immediately.

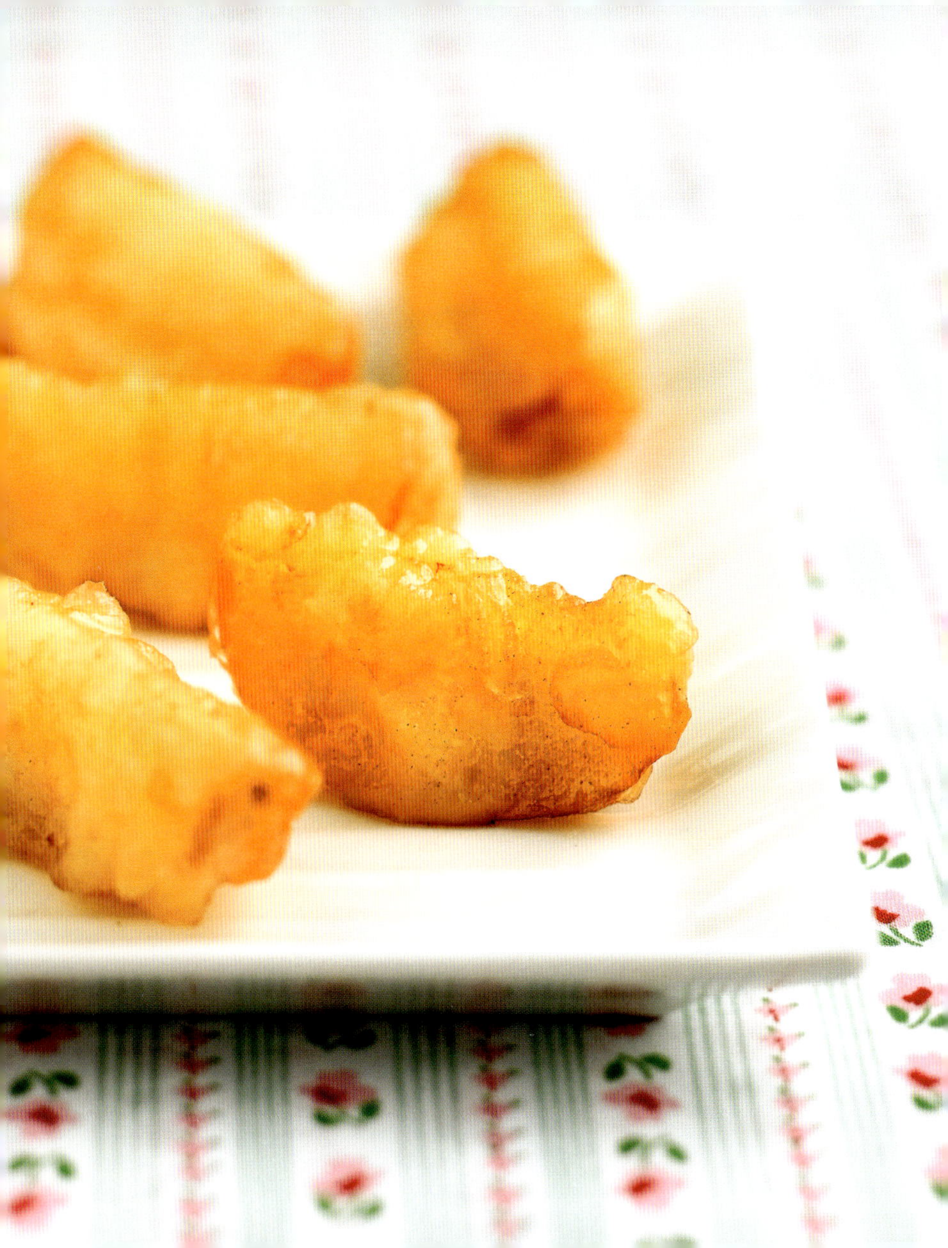

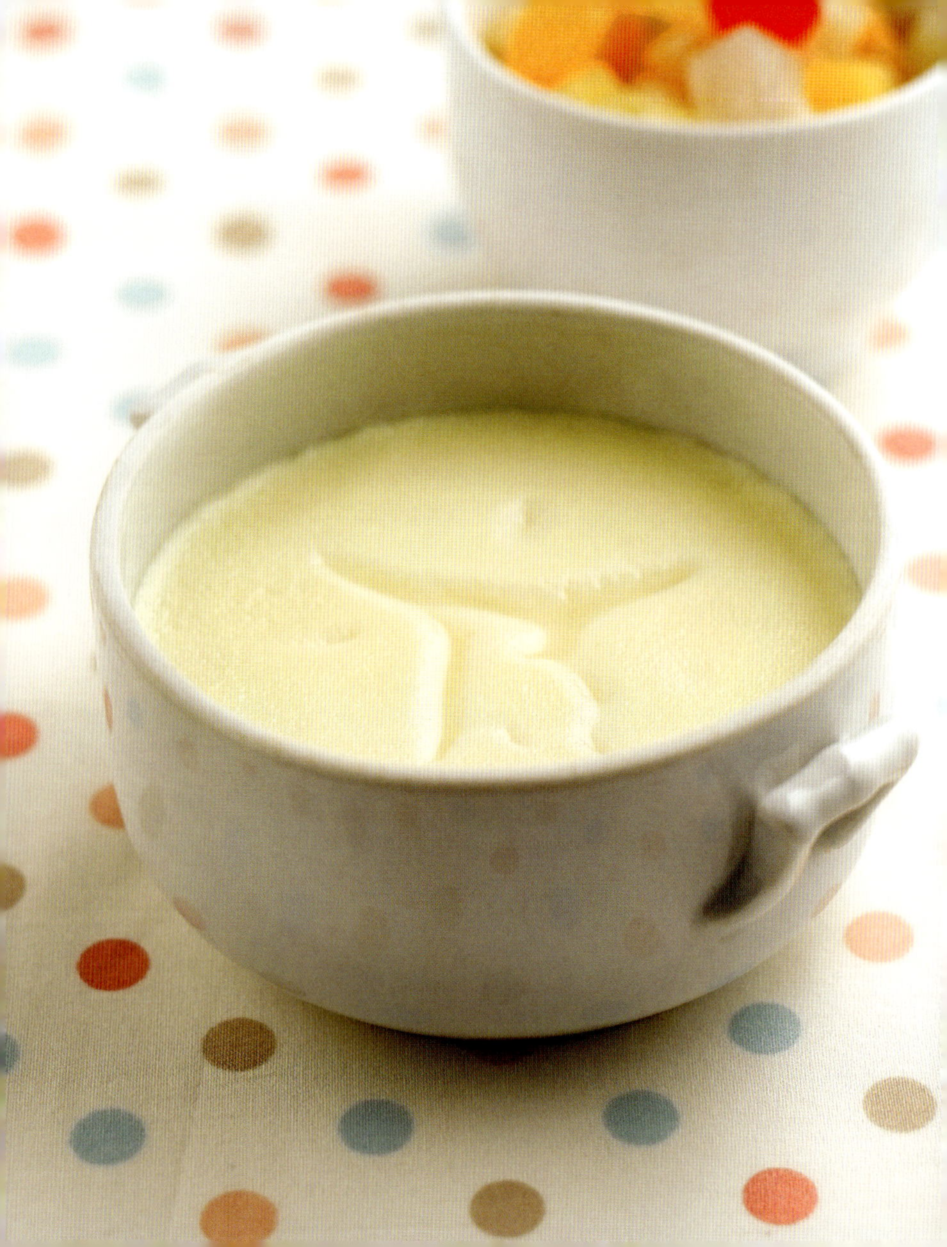

steamed milk egg Serves 1

This recipe makes enough for one helping. Multiply the quantities to make more as necessary.

NOTE

As a variation to this recipe, castor sugar may be substituted with 1 Tbsp honey. If using honey, heat milk to dissolve honey, then cool before adding to beaten egg.

INGREDIENTS

Egg	1, lightly beaten
Milk	180 ml (6 fl oz / $3/4$ cup)
Castor (superfine) sugar	1 Tbsp or to taste

METHOD

- Strain beaten egg into a bowl. Stir in milk and sugar, then pour mixture into a small steaming bowl.

- Place in a steamer and cover partially. Steam over gently boiling water for about 10 minutes until lightly set. Serve hot.

lotus root agar-agar Serves 4–6

The lotus root bits in the agar-agar add texture to this cool and refreshing dish. Serve as a sweet ending to a dim sum meal.

INGREDIENTS

Lotus root	1 section, peeled and cut into small pieces
Agar-agar powder	6 g ($1/5$ oz)
Castor (superfine) sugar	125 g ($4^{1}/_{2}$ oz)
Water	500 ml (16 fl oz / 2 cups)

METHOD

- Soak lotus root pieces in cold water for 30 minutes.
- Place agar-agar powder, castor sugar and water together in a pot. Simmer gently for 30 minutes, stirring until agar-agar powder and sugar are dissolved. Remove from heat.
- Drain lotus root pieces and add to agar-agar mixture. Pour mixture into a medium-size square pan and leave to cool. Cover with plastic wrap and refrigerate until set and chilled.
- Cut into small pieces and serve chilled.

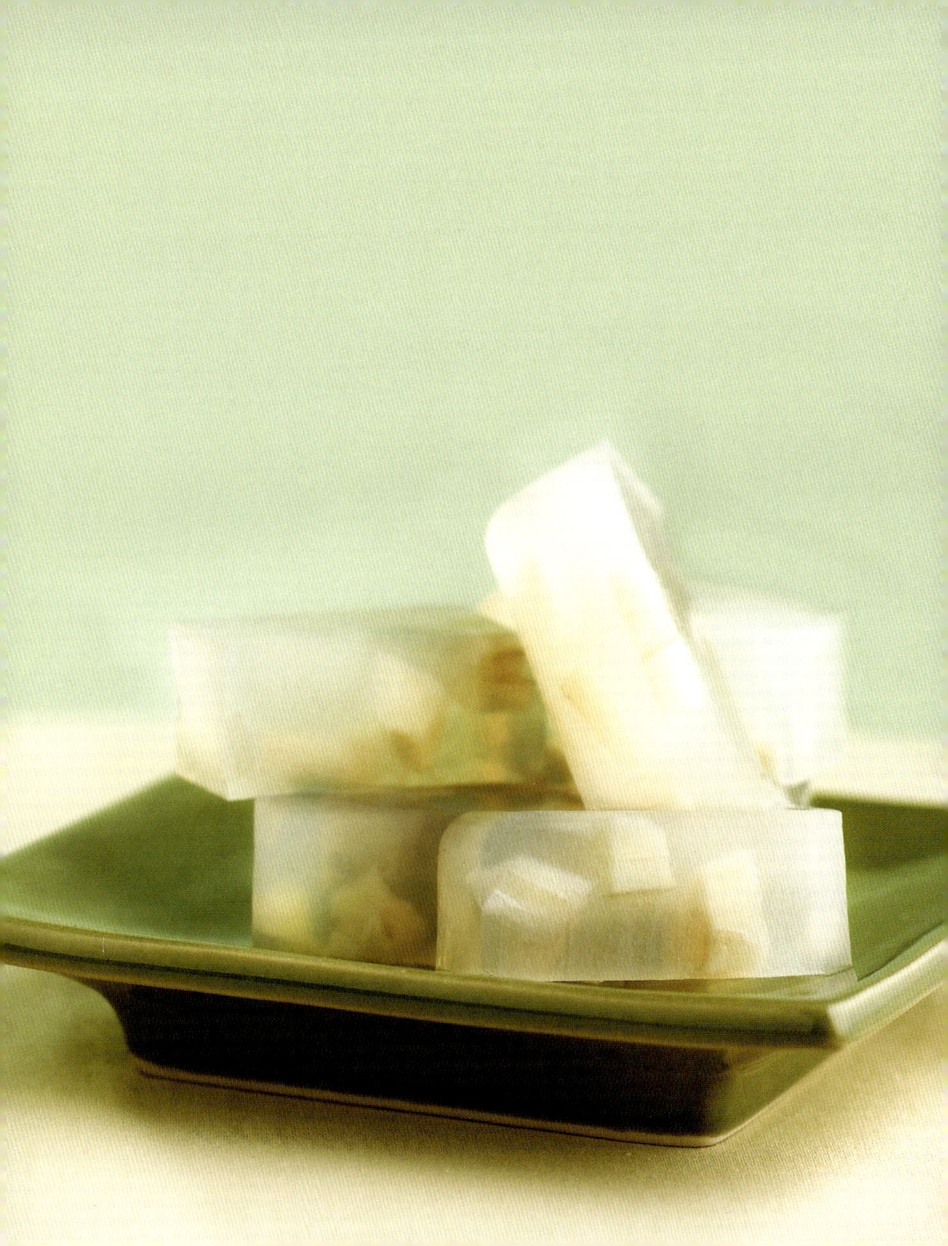

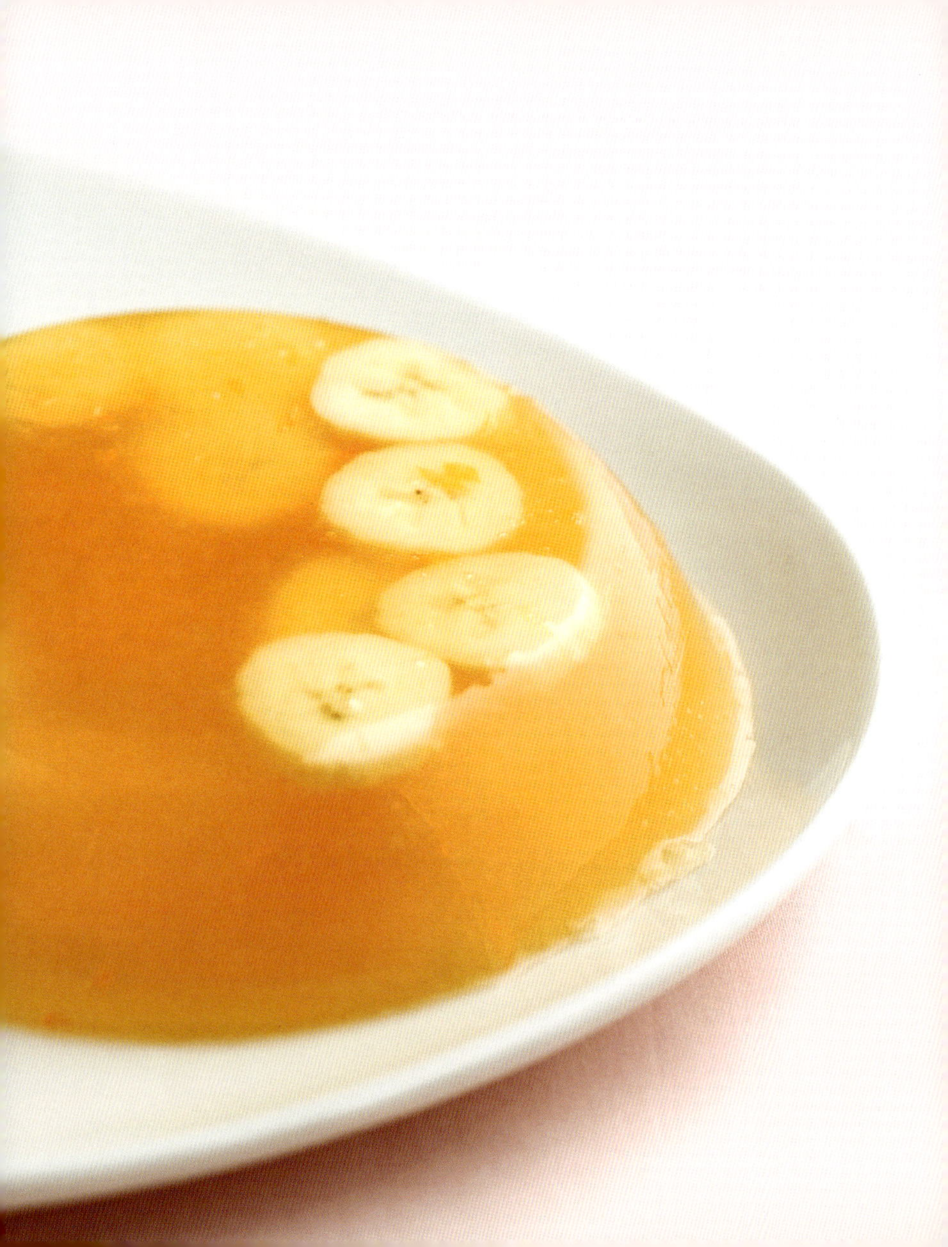

banana gelatine Serves 4–6

Slice the bananas just before placing in the mould and pouring the gelatine over, so they do not oxidise and take on an unattractive dark grey colour.

INGREDIENTS

Water	375 ml (12 fl oz / 1½ cups)
Unflavoured gelatine powder	25 g (1 oz)
Castor (superfine) sugar	110 g (4 oz)
Orange juice	125 ml (4 fl oz / ½ cup)
Lemon juice	2 Tbsp
Bananas	3

METHOD

- Pour 125 ml (4 fl oz / ½ cup) water into a bowl. Sprinkle gelatine over water and leave for 5 minutes. Bring remaining water to the boil and stir into gelatine mixture to dissolve gelatine.

- Add castor sugar, stirring until completely dissolved. Set aside for 10 minutes.

- Mix orange and lemon juices in a bowl and stir into gelatine mixture.

- Peel and slice bananas into rounds. Arrange in a medium-size dessert mould and pour a third of gelatine mixture over bananas. Refrigerate for 5 minutes.

- Add half of the remaining gelatine mixture to the mould and refrigerate for another 5 minutes. Finally, add remaining gelatine mixture. Refrigerate for 30 minutes to 1 hour until set.

- To remove gelatine from mould, place mould up to the rim in boiling water for 5–10 seconds, then invert mould onto a serving plate. Return to refrigerator to chill for 10 minutes before slicing to serve.

sweet-scented lychees Serves 4–6

A simple yet delightful way to dress up sweet lychees. Canned lychees work just as well as fresh ones in this recipe. The former also does away with the hassle of having to peel and stone fresh lychees.

INGREDIENTS

Sugar	70 g (2½ oz)
Water	75 ml (2½ fl oz / 5 Tbsp)
Ginger syrup	1 Tbsp
Lemon	1, zest finely grated and juice extracted
Dry white wine	75 ml (2½ fl oz / 5 Tbsp)
Lychees	450 g (1 lb), peeled and stoned, or drained if using canned lychees
Ginger	2.5-cm (1-in) knob, peeled and finely minced
Finely grated lime zest	1 Tbsp

METHOD

- Mix sugar with water in a saucepan. Stir over low heat for 3–5 minutes or until sugar dissolves.

- Add ginger syrup, lemon juice, wine and half the lemon zest. Bring to the boil.

- Add lychees, reduce to low heat and simmer for 5 minutes.

- Remove from heat and transfer lychees and syrup into a large bowl. Set aside to cool before placing in the refrigerator to chill for 2 hours.

- Stir in minced ginger and sprinkle with lime zest and remaining lemon zest just before serving.

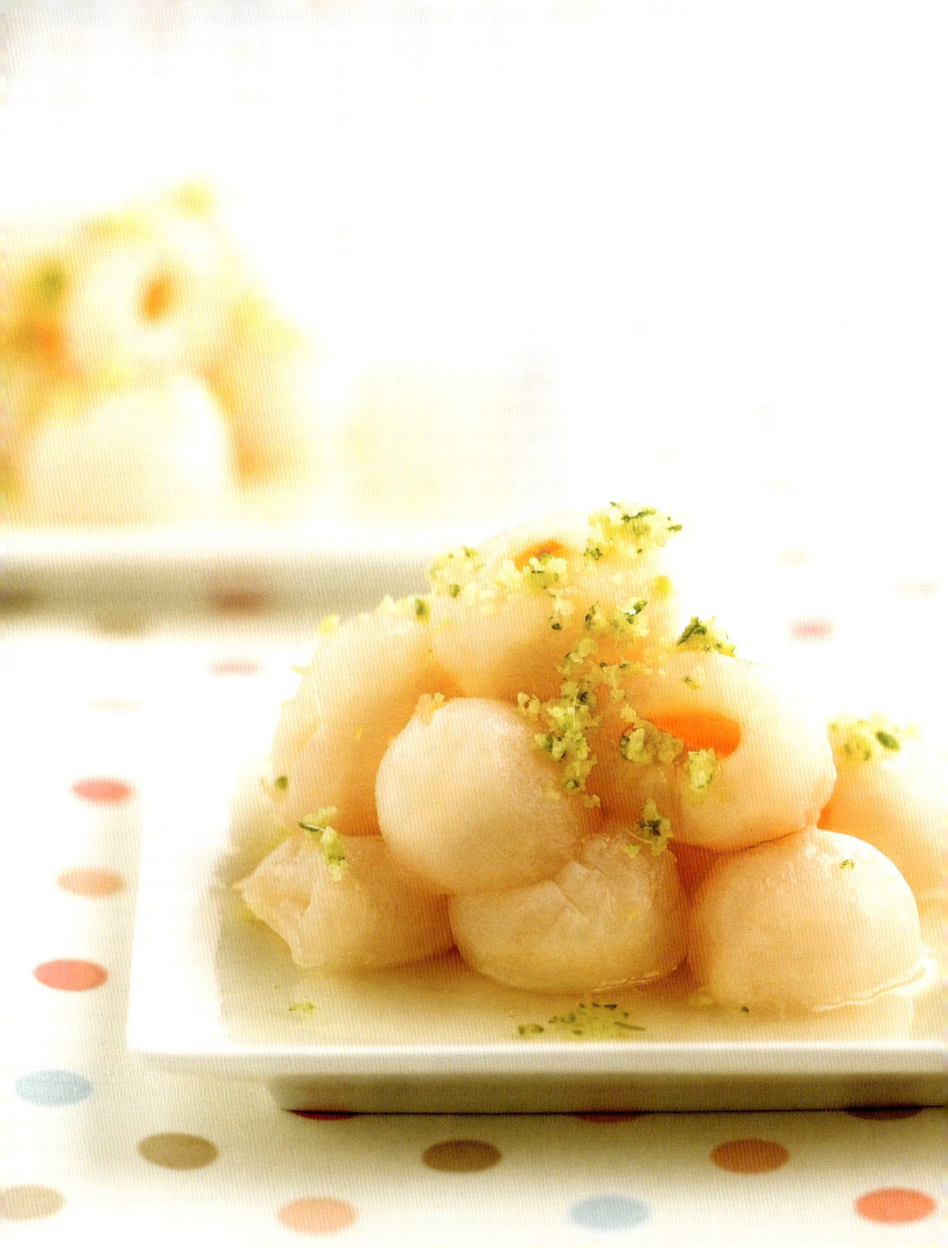

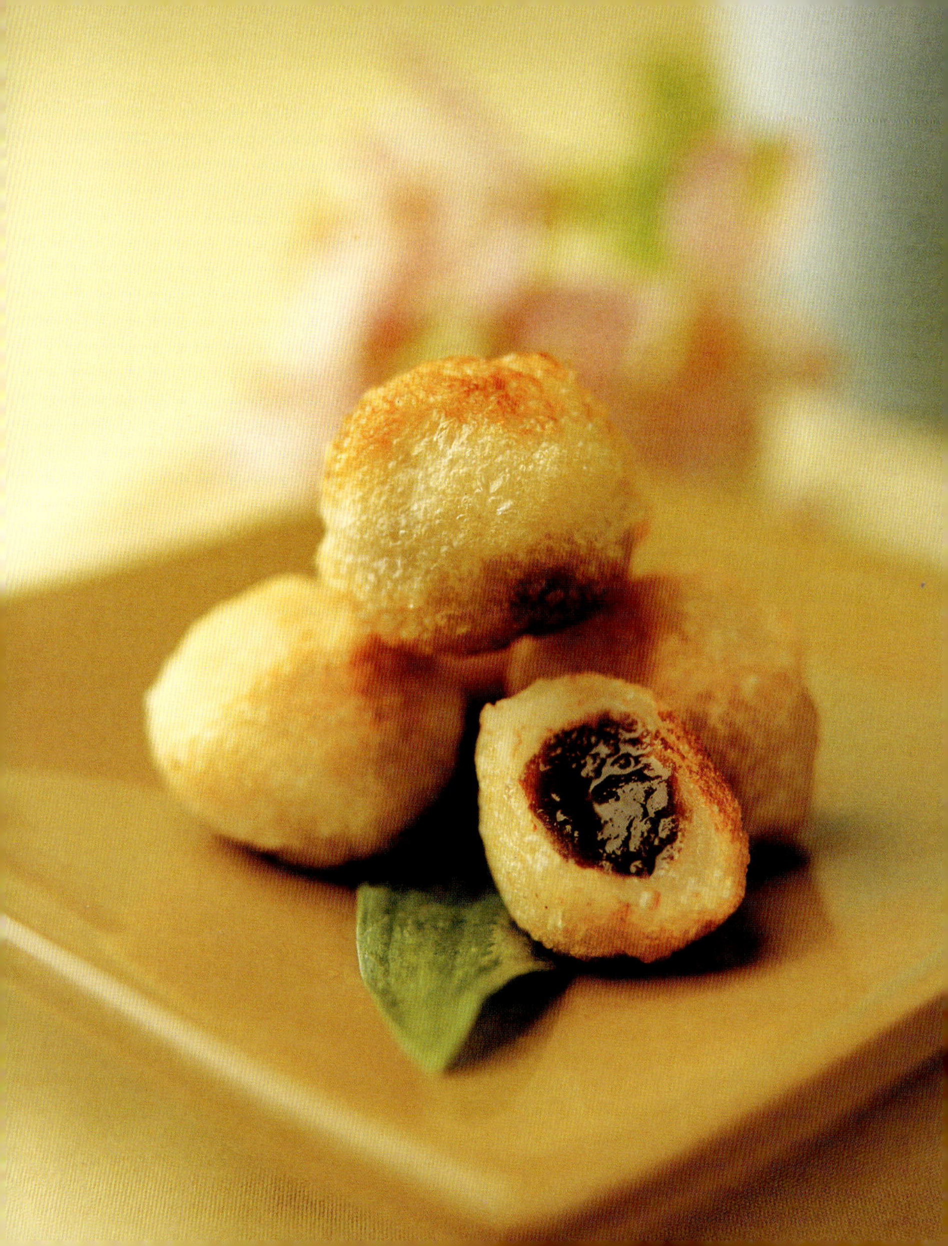

sweet dumplings Serves 4

These glutinous rice balls can also be enjoyed without frying, served in a syrup. Frying them, however, adds bite and texture.

INGREDIENTS

Cold water	200 ml (6½ fl oz)
Glutinous rice flour	225 g (8 oz)
Ready-made red bean paste	225 g (8 oz)
Vegetable oil	

NOTE
Ready-made red bean paste is available in some supermarkets. To make your own, refer to pages 32–33.

METHOD

- Gradually stir cold water into flour and work into a smooth dough. Add 1–2 Tbsp more water if necessary.

- Take a small piece of dough about the size of a chestnut and shape it into a round. Press a thumb into the round to create a depression.

- Insert 1 tsp red bean paste into dough and enclose. Roll dumpling between your palms to make it round. Repeat until dough and bean paste are used up.

- Bring 1.5 litres (48 fl oz / 6 cups) water to the boil in a large pot. Add dumplings, one by one, and allow water to return to the boil. Stir dumplings around in pot to prevent them from sticking to the pot. Reduce heat but leave water to boil for 5–6 minutes or until dumplings float to the surface.

- Remove dumplings with a slotted spoon to a warm serving plate.

- Heat some oil in a frying pan and fry dumplings in small batches over medium-low heat until golden brown. Dish out and serve hot.

glutinous rice with fruit Serves 6–8

This sweet rice pudding is a mixture of textures and tastes. You may also make it in small individual servings, if desired.

INGREDIENTS

Lotus seeds	60 g (2 oz)
Barley	60 g (2 oz)
Glutinous rice	280 g (10 oz)
Sugar	110 g (4 oz)
Cooking oil	1½ Tbsp
Red and green glacé cherries	60 g (2 oz), cut into small cubes
Dried red dates	25 g (1 oz), cut into small cubes
Preserved white melon strips	25 g (1 oz), cut into small cubes
Dried longan pulp	25 g (1 oz), cut into small cubes
Shelled melon seeds	25 g (1 oz)
Corn flour (cornstarch)	1 Tbsp, mixed with 2 Tbsp water

METHOD

- Place lotus seeds and barley into separate bowls. Add 2 Tbsp water into each bowl and steam for 30 minutes.

- Place glutinous rice in a bowl with half the sugar and 4 Tbsp water. Steam for 25 minutes.

- Lightly oil the inside of a medium-size bowl. Arrange lotus seeds, barley, cherries, red dates, preserved white melon strips, longan flesh and melon seeds all around the inside of the bowl. Spoon glutinous rice into the prepared bowl and steam for 10 minutes. Remove from heat and turn glutinous rice out onto a plate.

- Bring about 200 ml (6½ fl oz) water to the boil and stir in remaining sugar. Stir in corn flour mixture to thicken syrup, then pour over glutinous rice. Serve.

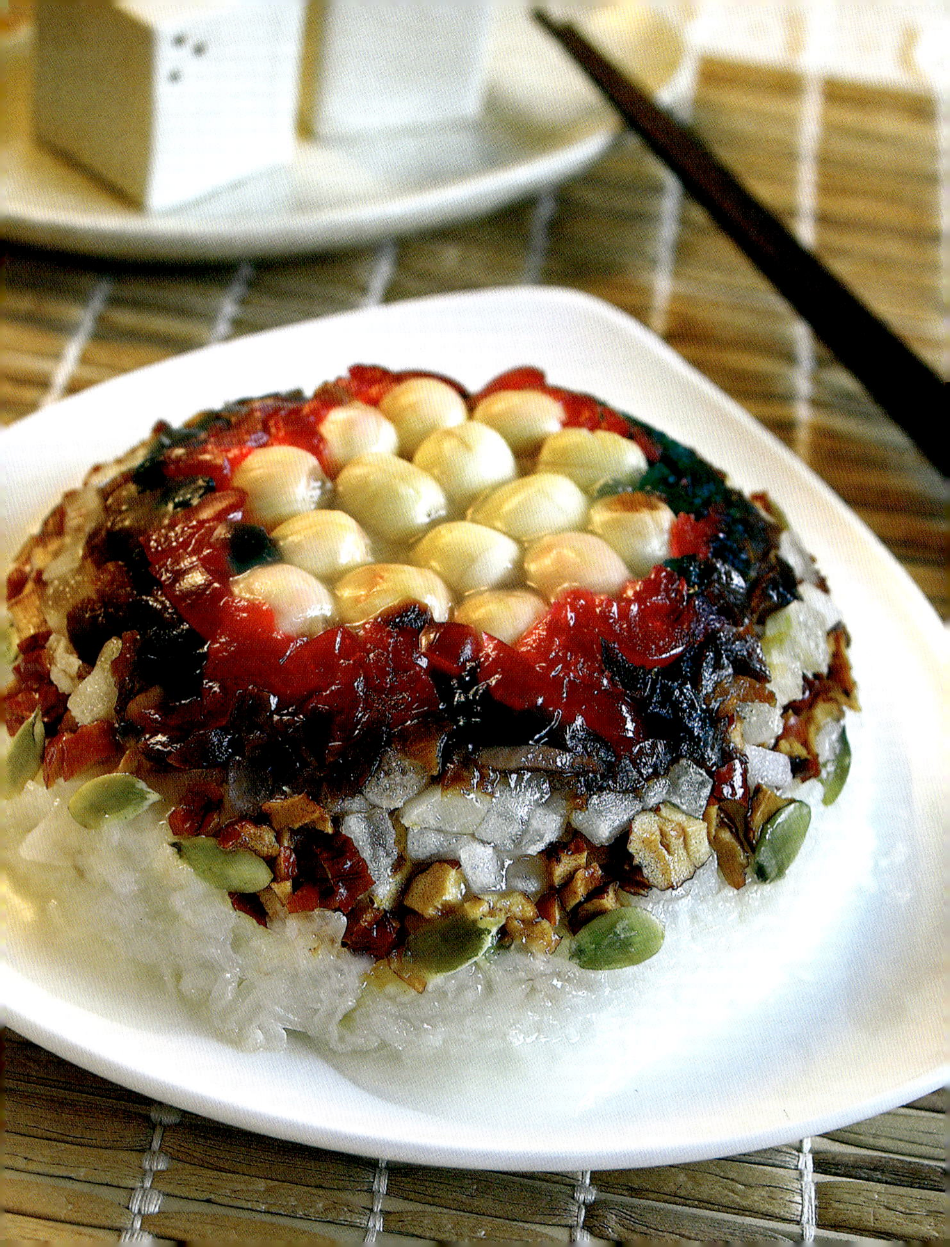

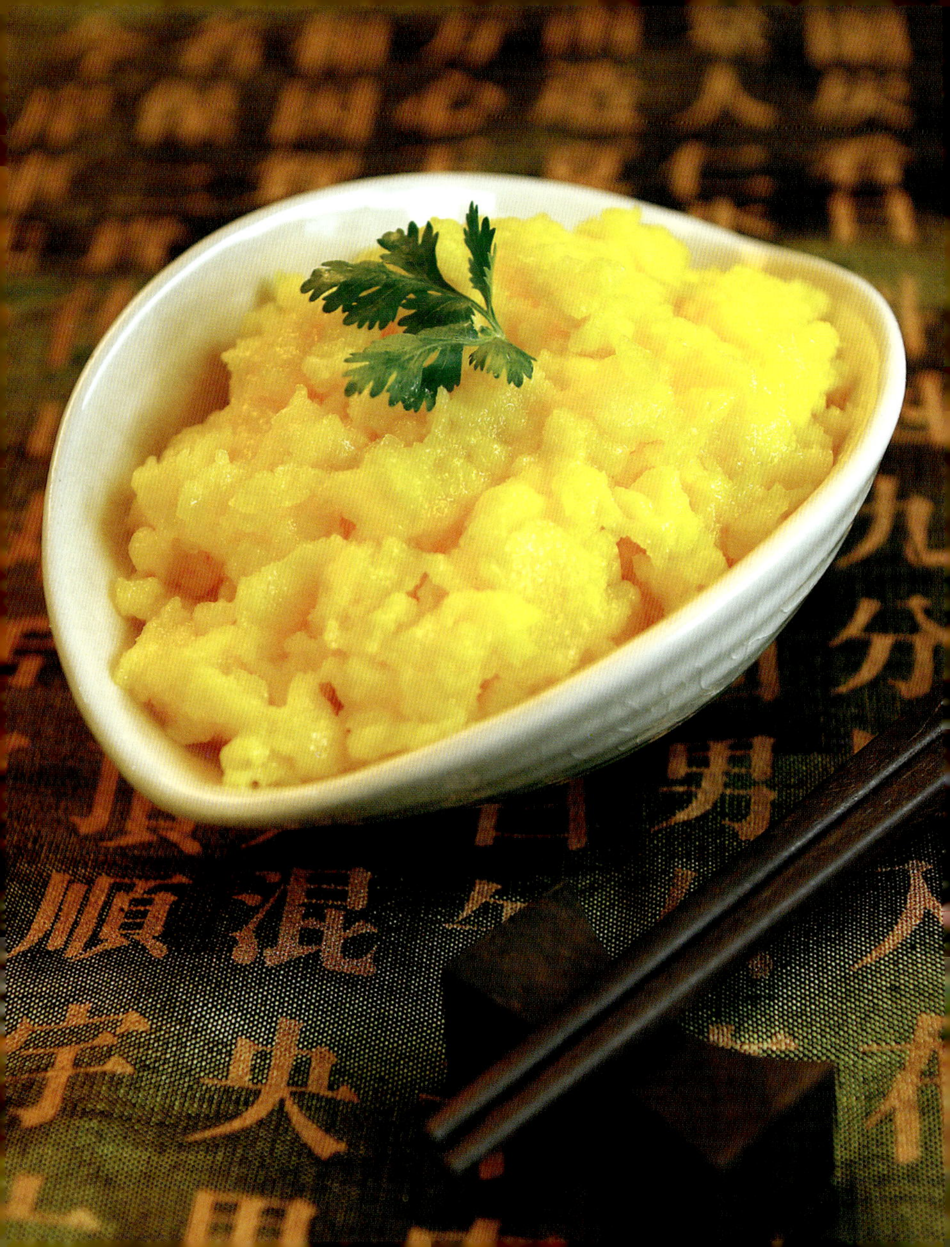

stir-fried egg yolks Serves 6

The egg yolks give this dish a bright and vibrant colour. The key to making this dish well is to cook it slowly over low heat.

INGREDIENTS

Egg yolks	6
Eggs	2
Sugar	120 g (4 1/2 oz)
Water	3 Tbsp
Corn flour (cornstarch)	2 Tbsp, mixed with 3 Tbsp water
Cooking oil	90 ml (3 fl oz / 6 Tbsp)

METHOD

- Combine egg yolks, eggs, sugar, water and corn flour mixture in a bowl. Mix well.

- Heat half the oil in a pan over low heat. Gradually pour in egg paste and cook over low heat while stirring and drizzling in remaining oil until egg paste no longer sticks to wok.

- Dish out and garnish as desired. Serve.

sweet yam paste (au nee) Serves 4

This adaptation of the traditional Teochew dessert of mashed yam has gingko nuts and pumpkin cubes for extra texture and flavour.

INGREDIENTS

Sugar	280 g (10 oz)
Pumpkin	220 g (8 oz), peeled and cut into small cubes
Yam	900 g (2 lb), peeled and cut into small cubes
Lard	6 Tbsp
Shallots	3, peeled and sliced thinly
Canned gingko nuts	115 g (4 oz)

METHOD

- Heat 2 Tbsp water in a shallow pan over low heat. Add 100 g ($3^1/_2$ oz) sugar and stir to melt sugar. Add pumpkin cubes and cook until sugar is absorbed. Add more water as necessary while cooking to prevent sugar from burning. Set pumpkin cubes aside.

- Steam yam pieces over rapidly boiling water until very soft. Place half the yam in a food processor with 2 Tbsp lard and half the remaining sugar until paste is smooth. Remove to a bowl and repeat with remaining yam.

- Heat remaining 2 Tbsp lard in a wok and fry sliced shallots until lightly browned. Add yam paste and stir-fry over low heat for 30 seconds, mixing well with shallots.

- Divide yam paste into serving bowls and top with pumpkin cubes and gingko nuts. Serve hot.

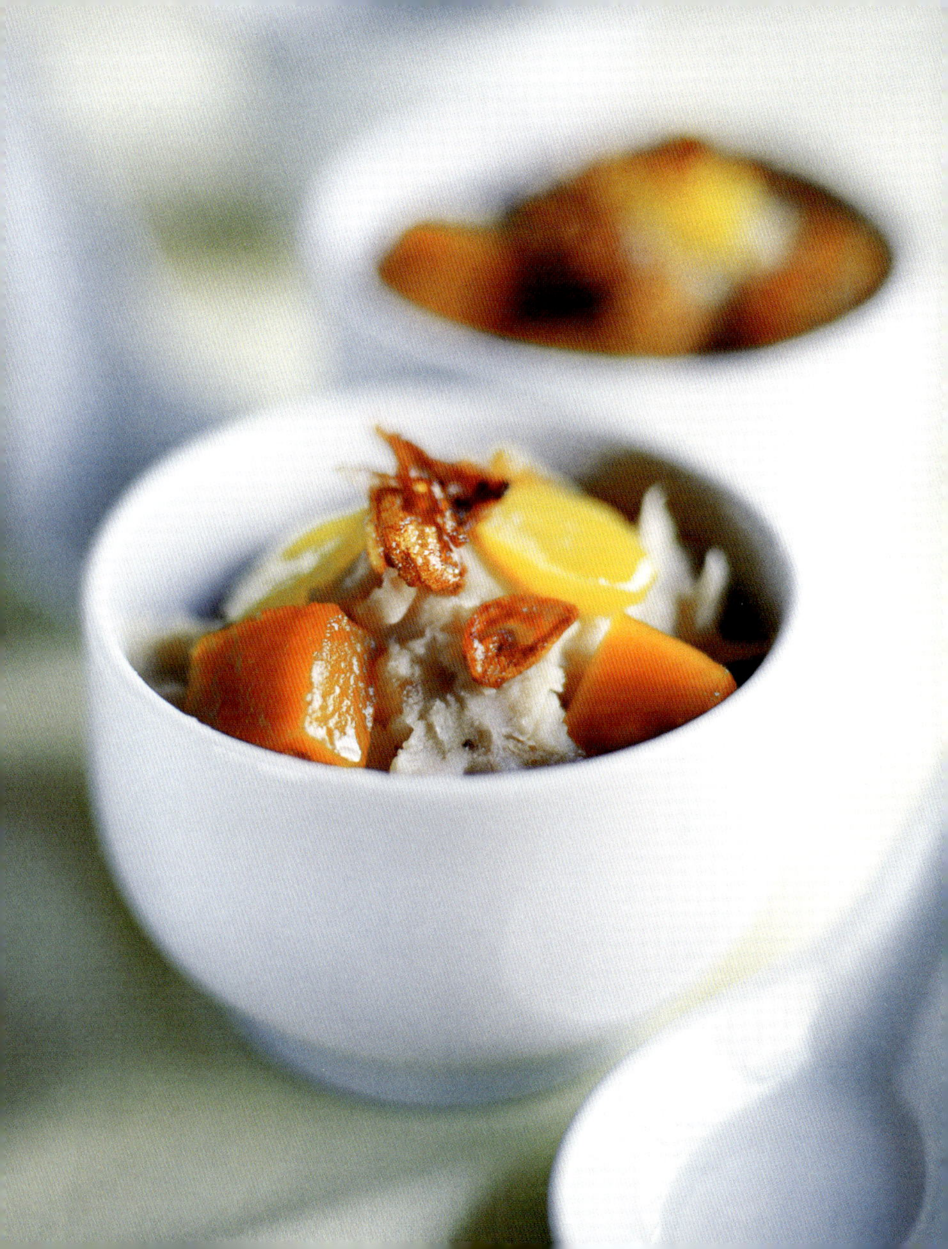

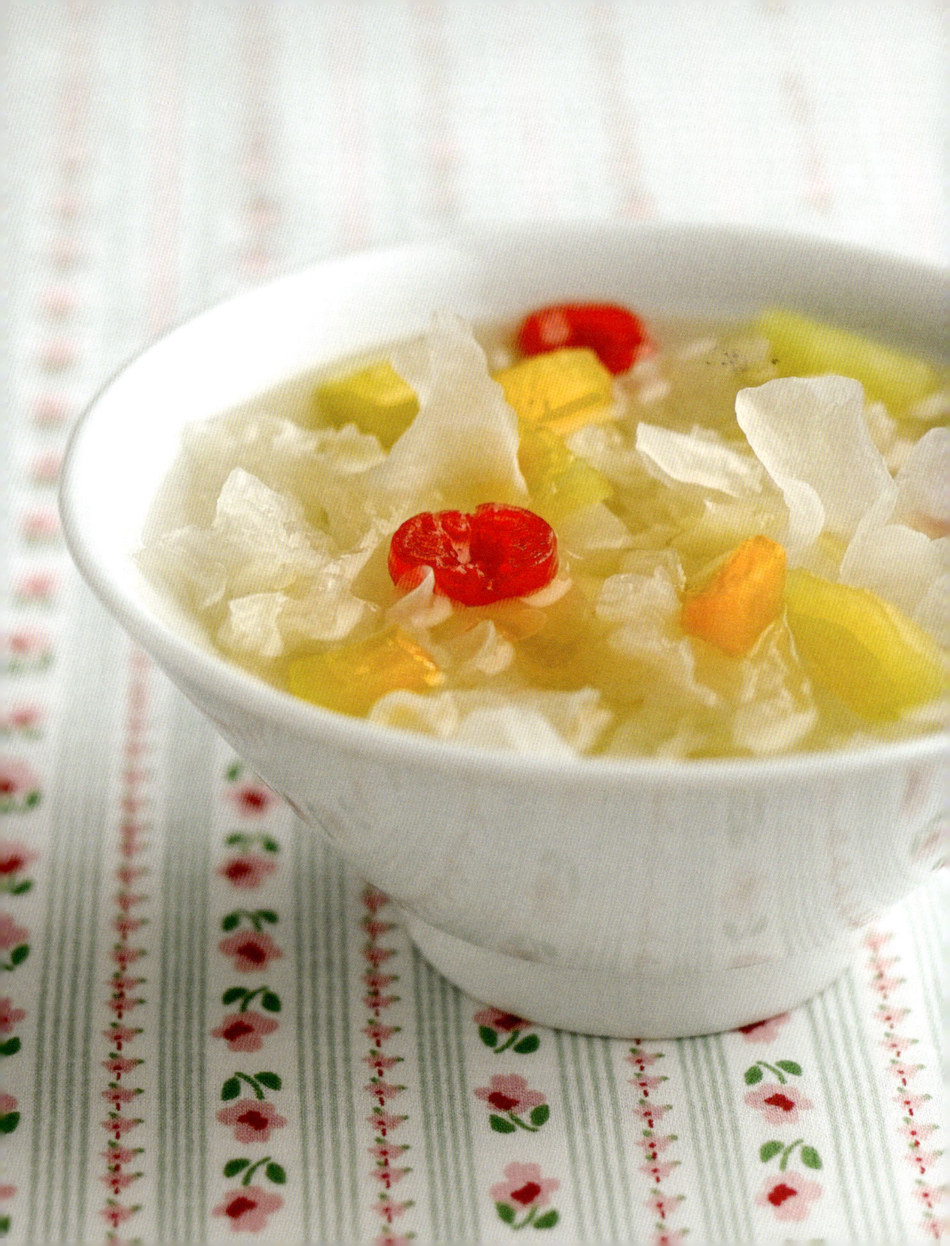

white fungus dessert Serves 4

White fungus is said to contain iron, calcium and vitamin C, and is also believed to be good for the skin. Enjoy this tasty dessert that is also full of health benefits!

INGREDIENTS

Dried white fungus	30 g (1 oz), soaked in warm water for 1 hour until slightly expanded
Rock sugar	70 g (2 1/2 oz)
Water	1 litre (32 fl oz / 4 cups)
Canned fruit cocktail	450 g (1 lb), drained

METHOD

- Place white fungus and rock sugar in a pot with water. Bring to the boil, then lower heat and simmer gently for 30 minutes.
- Remove from heat. Let cool slightly, then add fruit cocktail.
- Serve immediately if serving hot, or allow to cool before refrigerating for at least 1 hour if serving cold.

lily bulb petals with lotus seeds Serves 4

This light and refreshing Chinese dessert can be easily prepared and served as a snack at anytime of the day.

NOTE
Ready-to-use lotus seeds in vacuum packs are now conveniently available at supermarkets or Chinese grocery stores. If using dried lotus seeds, soak overnight before use.

INGREDIENTS

Water	1 litre (32 fl oz / 4 cups)
Dried lily bulb petals	100 g ($3^1/_2$ oz), soaked overnight
Lotus seeds	225 g (8 oz)
Rock sugar	70 g ($2^1/_2$ oz)

METHOD

- Bring water, lily bulb petals, lotus seeds and rock sugar to the boil in a pot. Stir to dissolve sugar.
- Lower heat, cover and simmer for 40 minutes until ingredients are soft.
- Ladle into serving bowls and serve hot.

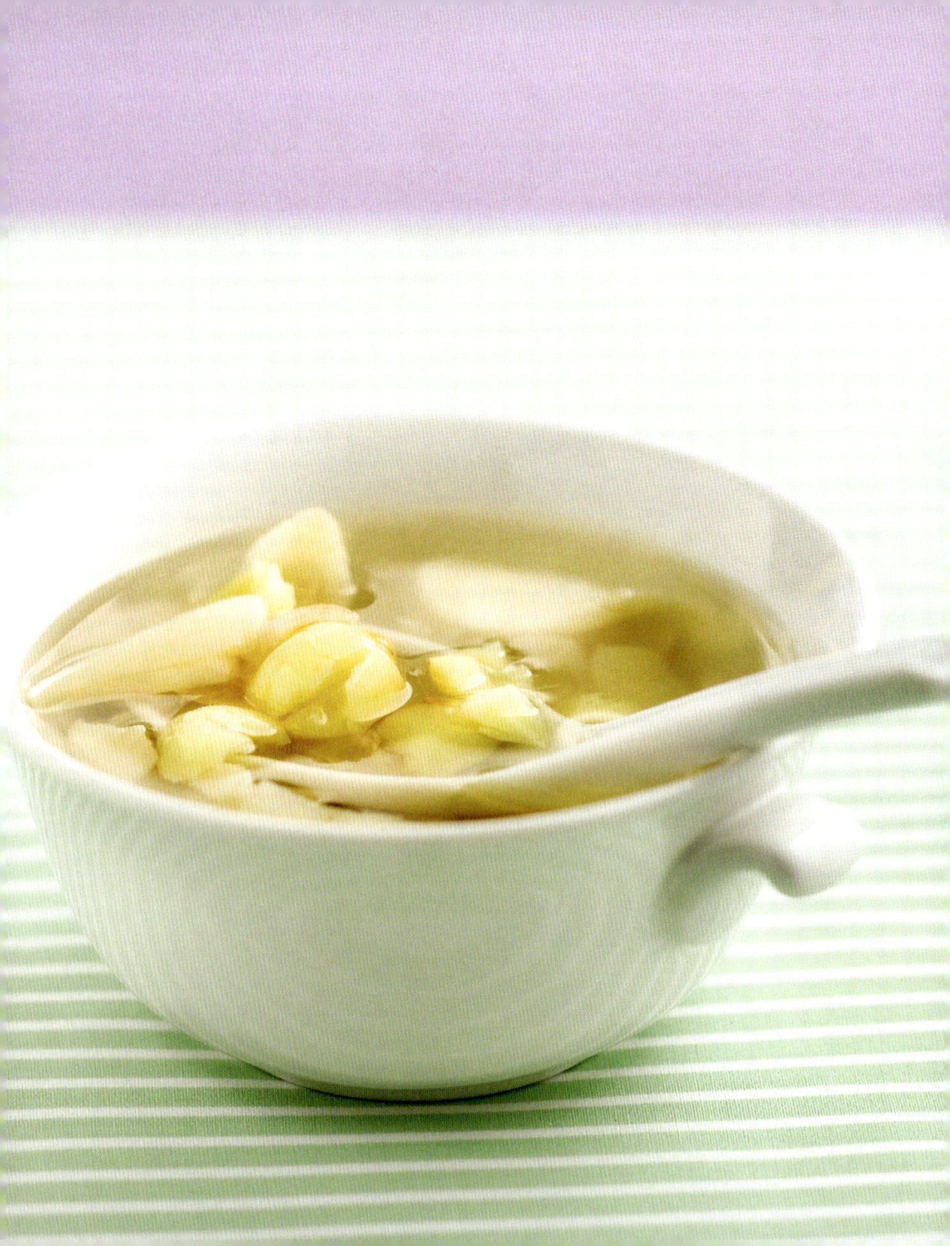

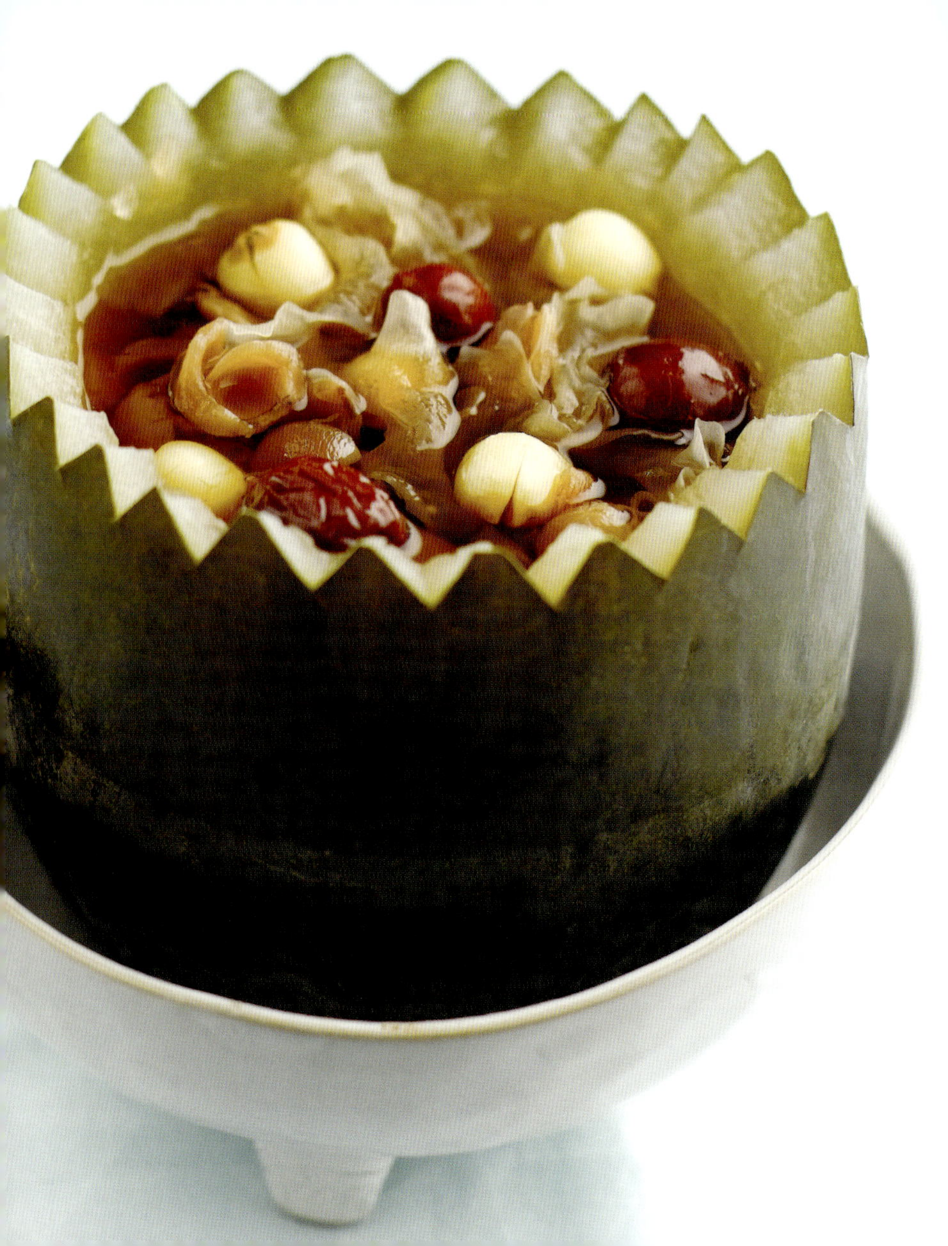

winter melon delight Serves 4–6

Besides refreshing the palate, this Chinese dessert prepared with red dates, white fungus and lotus seeds is also a wonderful health tonic.

INGREDIENTS

Winter melon	1.5–2 kg (3 lb 4$^1\!/_2$ oz–4 lb 6 oz)
Rock sugar	85 g (3 oz)
Dried red dates	6, soaked in cold water, seeded and slit
Dried longan	2 tsp
Lotus seeds (page 56)	100 g (3$^1\!/_2$ oz)
Dried white fungus	30 g (1 oz), soaked in warm water for 1 hour until slightly expanded
Boiling water	750 ml (24 fl oz / 3 cups)

METHOD

- Slice top stem end off winter melon and discard. Decorate rim of melon with a zig-zag cut all around. Scoop out seeds and pith, and rinse melon with boiling water.

- Stand melon in a shallow heatproof bowl to hold it steady and upright. Place rock sugar, red dates and longan inside melon. Add boiling water. The water level should almost reach the rim.

- Place melon in a steamer. Cover and steam over gently boiling water for 45 minutes. Add lotus seeds and white fungus into melon. Replace lid of steamer and steam for another 20–30 minutes.

- Serve hot, using melon as a soup tureen.

lotus root with red dates Serves 4

Lotus root is commonly used in the preparation of savoury soups. Used in a sweet dessert such as this one, it takes on a different persona, but retains its lovely crunchy texture.

INGREDIENTS

Lotus root	2 sections, peeled and thinly sliced
Dried red dates	70 g ($2^1/_2$ oz), soaked in cold water and seeded
Rock sugar	70 g ($2^1/_2$ oz)
Water	1 litre (32 fl oz / 4 cups)

METHOD

- Wash lotus root slices thoroughly in salted water. Drain and set aside.
- Put lotus root slices into a pot with dates, rock sugar and water. Bring to the boil, then lower heat, cover and simmer for 1 hour or until mixture smells sweet. Add more water if necessary.
- Ladle into serving bowls and serve hot.

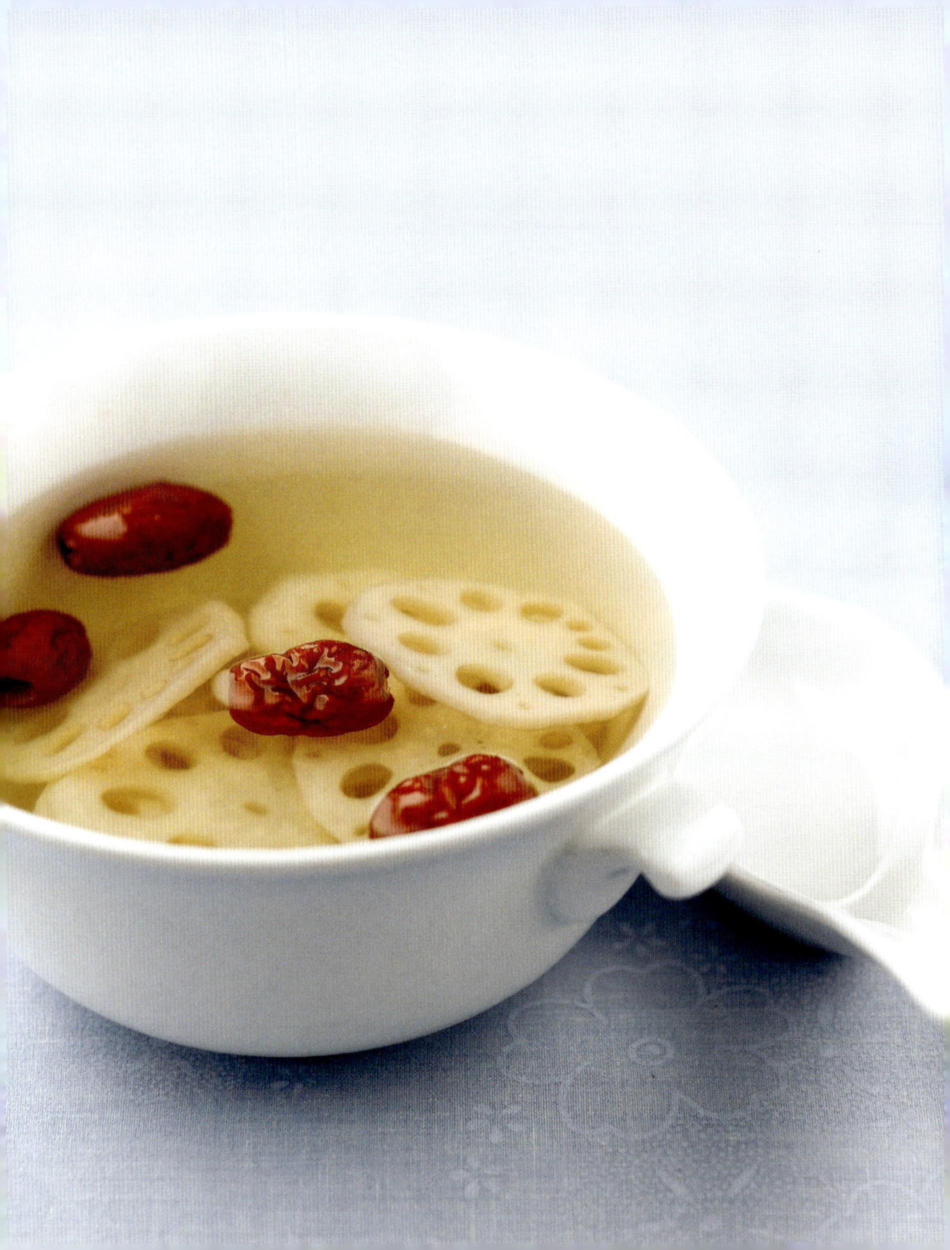

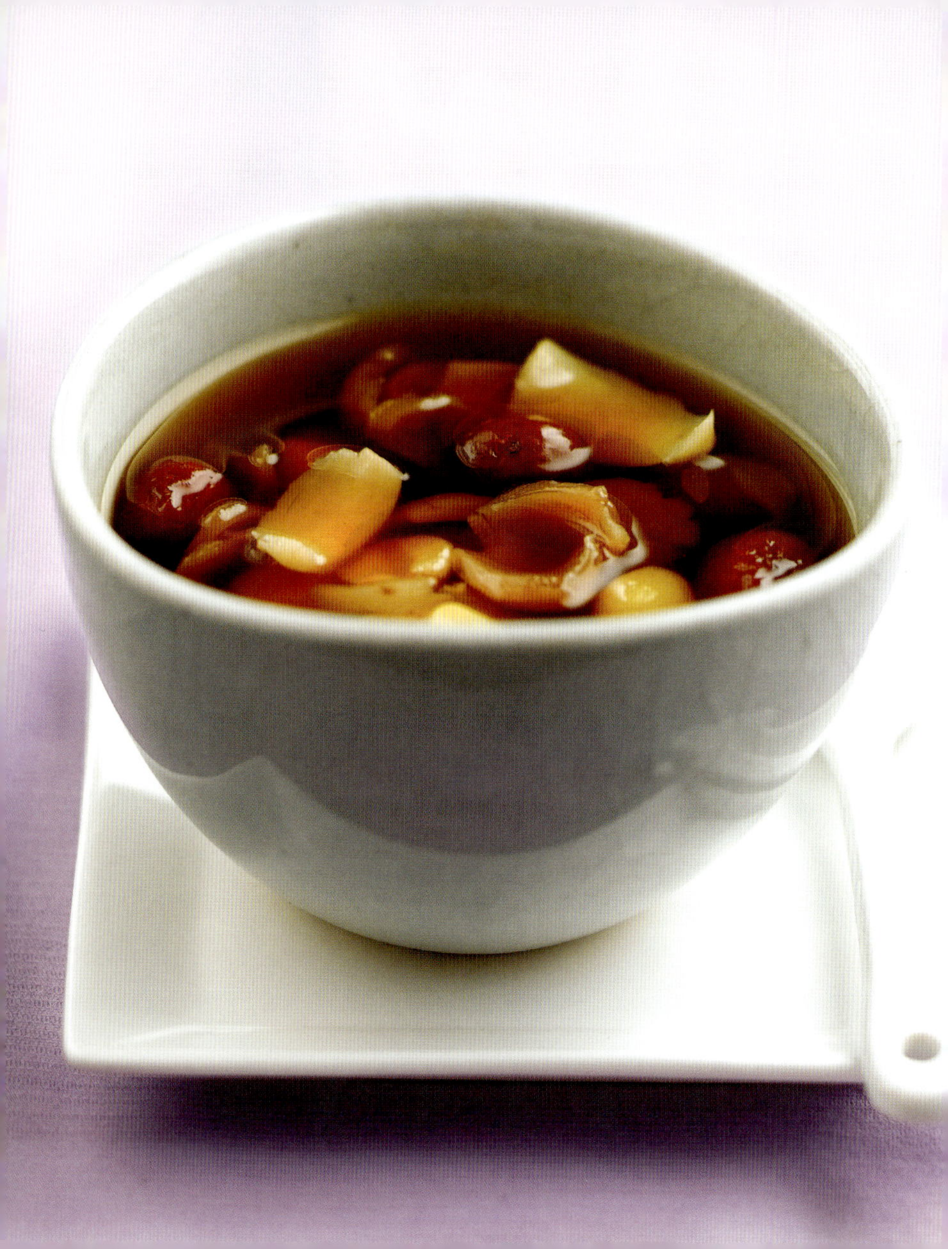

longan dessert with gingko nuts Serves 4

To remove bitter shoots in gingko nuts, gently push a toothpick through the centre of each nut.

INGREDIENTS

Ginkgo nuts	55 g (2 oz), skinned, bitter shoots removed
Dried longan	70 g (2$^1\!/_2$ oz)
Dried red dates	45 g (1$^1\!/_2$ oz), soaked in cold water and seeded
Lotus seeds	55 g (2 oz)
Dried lily bulb petals	55 g (2 oz), soaked in cold water for 2–3 hours and drained
Water	1.25 litres (40 fl oz / 5 cups)
Rock sugar	100 g (3$^1\!/_2$ oz)

NOTE
Ready-to-use gingko nuts and lotus seeds in vacuum packs or cans are now conveniently available at most supermarkets and Chinese grocery stores. Simply rinse before use.

METHOD

- Put all ingredients together in a pot. Bring to the boil, then lower heat, cover and simmer for 1 hour.
- Ladle into serving bowls and serve hot.

peanut crème Serves 4

This fragrant peanut dessert offers a perfect sweet ending to a meal. It can also be served as a snack at any time of the day.

INGREDIENTS

Roasted skinned peanuts	625 g (1 lb 6 oz)
Long grain rice	2 Tbsp, washed and drained
Water	2 litres (64 fl oz / 8 cups)
Sugar	300 g (11 oz)
Brown sugar (optional)	

METHOD

- Place half the peanuts, 1 Tbsp rice and 500 ml (16 fl oz / 2 cups) water in a blender and process until very fine. Transfer to a heavy-bottomed pan and set aside. Repeat with remaining half of peanuts, rice and another 500 ml (16 fl oz / 2 cups) water.

- Bring mixture to the boil over moderate heat, stirring continuously. Lower heat and simmer for another 5 minutes, stirring continuously. Remove from heat.

- Ladle into individual serving bowls and sprinkle some brown sugar over, if desired before serving hot.

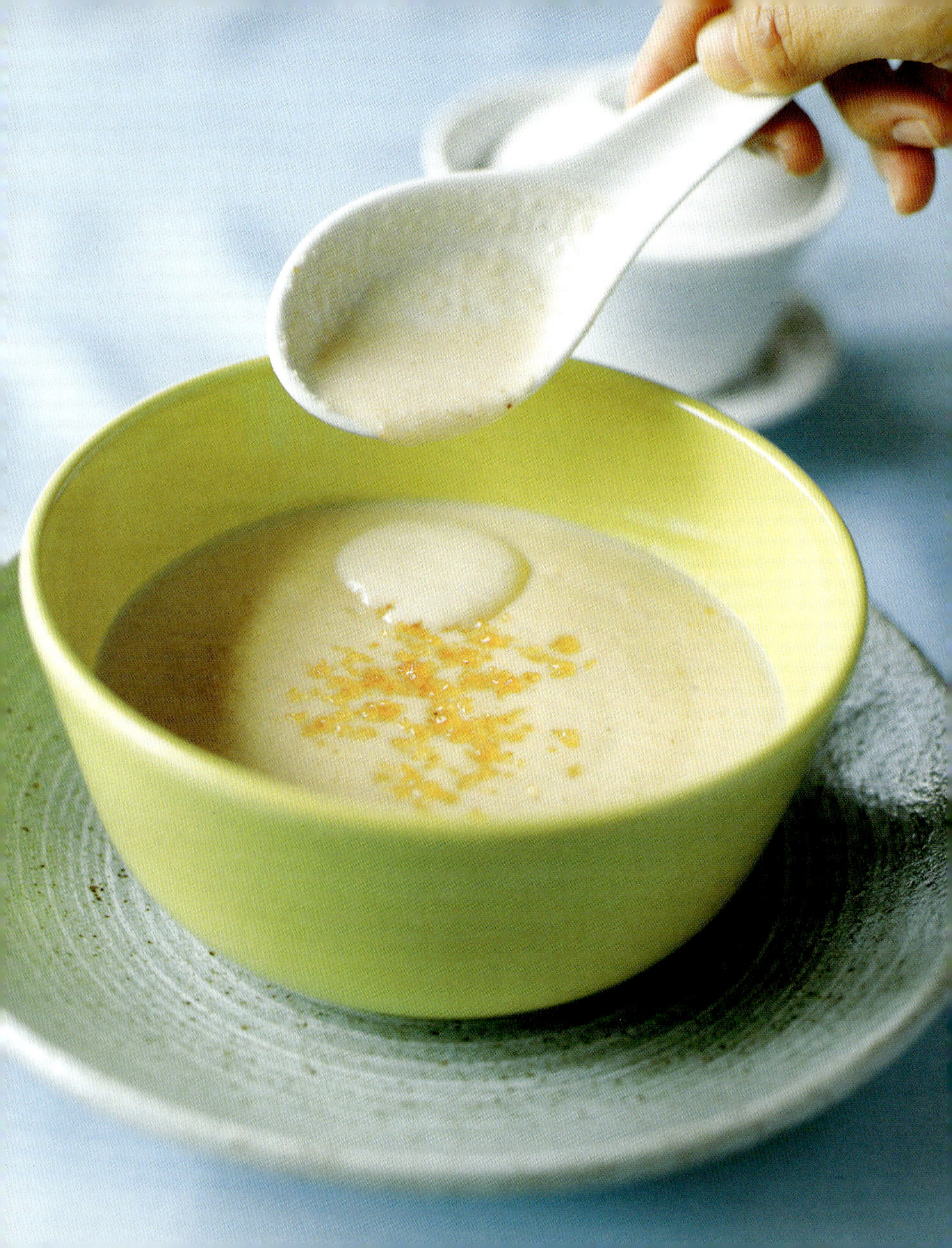

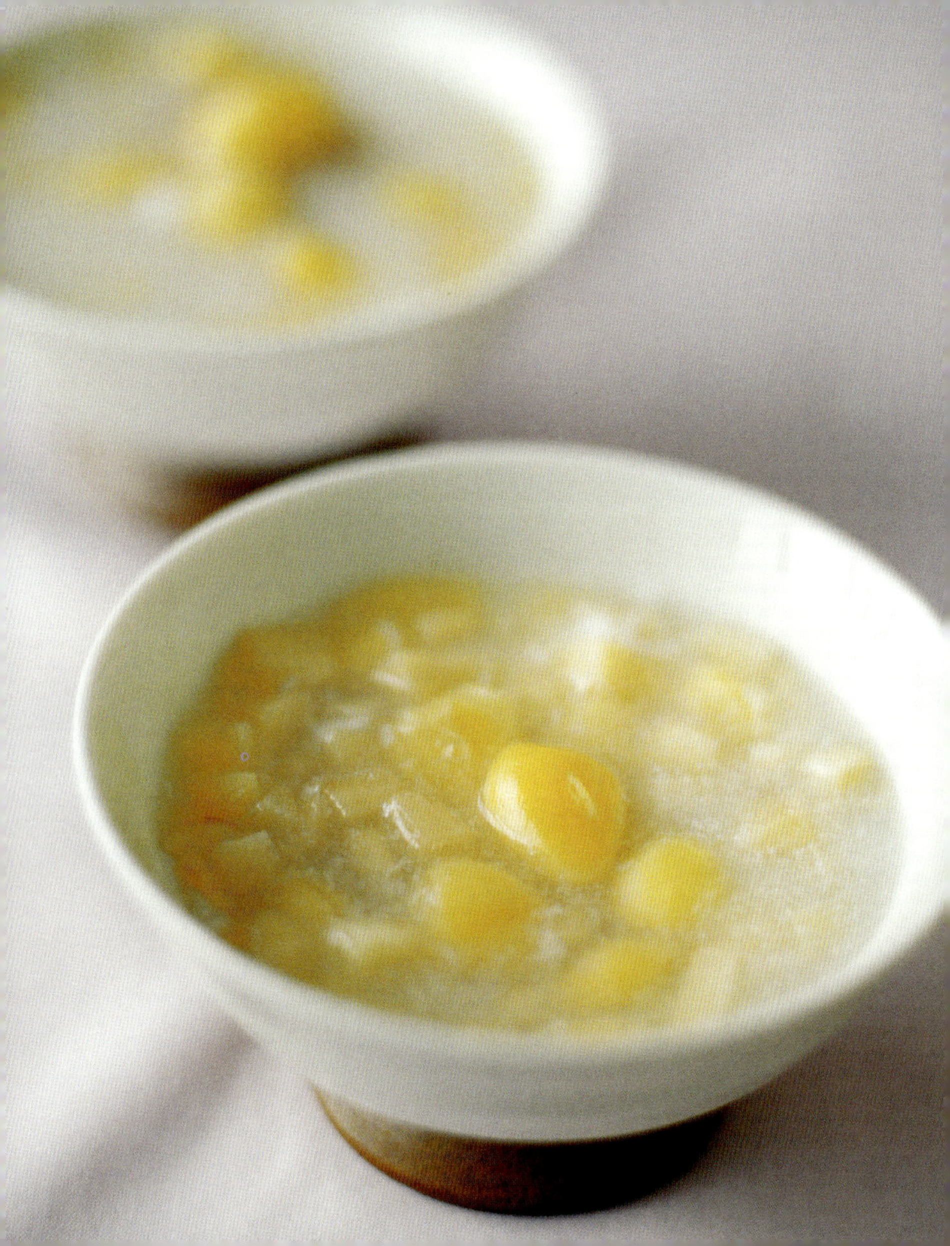

gingko nut and water chestnut dessert Serves 4

This sweet dessert made with gingko nuts and water chestnuts is delicious and refreshing.

INGREDIENTS

Water	1.5 litres (48 fl oz / 6 cups)
Rock sugar	300 g (11 oz)
Gingko nuts	180 g (6 oz), shelled and bitter centres removed
Water chestnuts	20, peeled and cut into 0.5-cm ($1/4$-in) cubes
Egg whites	2, lightly beaten
Sweet potato flour	3 Tbsp
Corn flour (cornstarch)	1 Tbsp
Water	125 ml (4 fl oz / $1/2$ cup)

METHOD

- Bring water to the boil in a large saucepan. Lower heat and add rock sugar, stirring occasionally. When sugar dissolves, add gingko nuts and continue to cook over low heat for 10 minutes. Add water chestnuts and simmer for another 10 minutes.

- Combine sweet potato flour, corn flour and water in a small bowl. Strain mixture and set aside.

- Slowly drizzle egg white into soup. Stir to prevent egg from cooking in clumps. Repeat with sweet potato flour solution. Allow water to return to the boil, then remove from heat.

- Serve hot or cold.

mung bean soup Serves 4

This Chinese dessert soup can be served both hot and cold. Adjust the amount of sugar used to your personal preference.

INGREDIENTS

Water	1.25 litres (40 fl oz / 5 cups)
Dried orange peel	1 piece, small
Mung beans	125 g (4$^{1}/_{2}$ oz), soaked overnight and drained
Canned lotus seeds	55 g (2 oz)
Brown sugar	50 g (2 oz)

NOTE

Use fresh orange zest as a substitute if dried orange peel is unavailable. The zest will add a refreshing tangy citrus flavour to the dish. Omit if desired.

METHOD

- Place water and orange peel in a pot and bring to the boil over moderately high heat.

- Reduce heat, add beans and lotus seeds and simmer, partially covered, for 1 hour or until beans are soft.

- Add sugar, stirring constantly until sugar dissolves.

- Ladle into serving bowls and serve immediately. If serving cold, leave to cool slightly before refrigerating for about 1 hour.

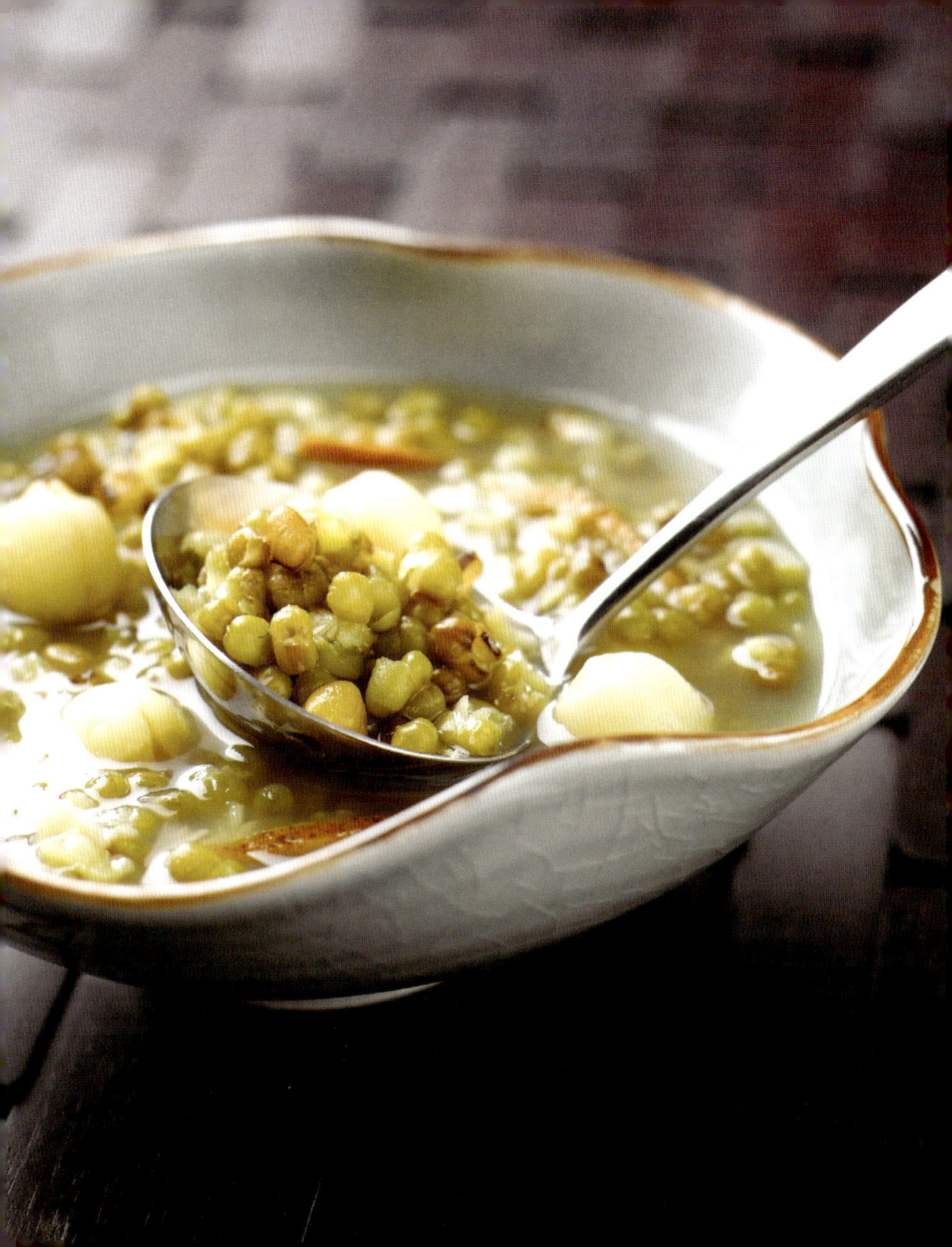

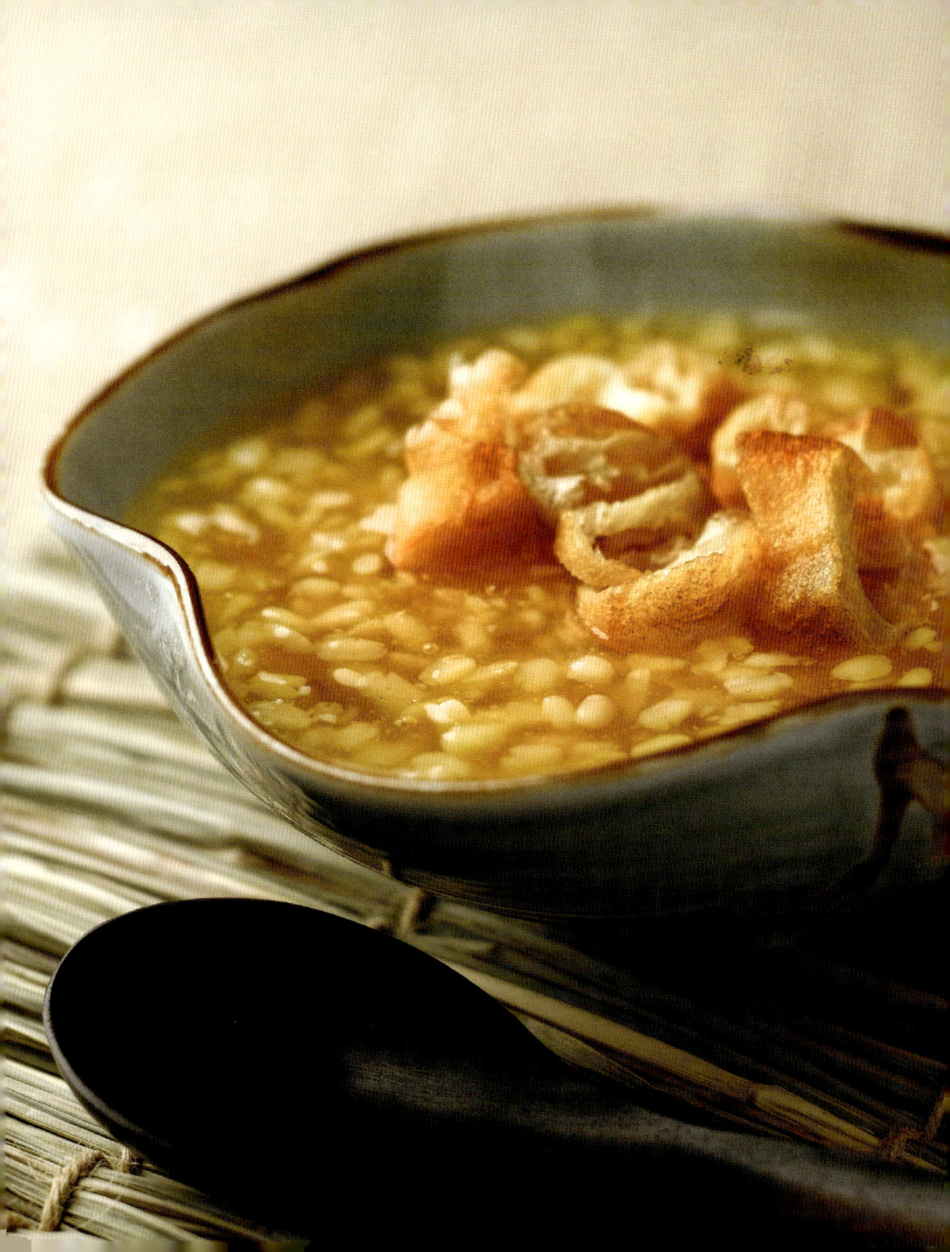

mung bean dessert Serves 8

This popular dessert is also known as *tau suan*. Serve hot.

INGREDIENTS

Split mung bean (green gram)	300 g (11 oz), soaked for 1 hour and drained
Screwpine (*pandan*) leaves	2, washed and knotted
Sugar	100 g (3½ oz)
Water	1 litre (32 fl oz / 4 cups)
Sweet potato flour	80 g (3 oz), sifted and mixed with 250 ml (8 fl oz / 1 cup) water
Dough fritters (*you tiao*) (optional)	2, sliced

METHOD

- Steam beans over boiling water for about 30 minutes or until beans are soft. Set aside.

- Add screwpine leaves, sugar and water to a pot. Bring to the boil, then reduce heat and stir in sweet potato mixture and mung beans. Stir until mixture thickens.

- Ladle into individual serving bowls and top with dough fritters, if desired. Serve hot.

fu chok tong shui Serves 4

This Chinese dessert is delicious when served hot, and refreshing when served cold. Adjust the amount of sugar added to your personal preference.

NOTE

Using canned ginkgo nuts is convenient as it does away with the need to shell the fresh nuts, soak them and remove their skins and bitter shoots.

INGREDIENTS

Bean curd sticks	180 g (6 oz), soaked to soften and drained
Canned ginkgo nuts	30
Rock sugar	125 g (4½ oz)
Water	1 litre (32 fl oz / 4 cups)
Eggs	2, lightly beaten

METHOD

- Cut soaked bean curd sticks into shorter lengths and place in a pot.
- Add all other ingredients, except eggs.
- Bring to the boil and simmer for about 1 hour 30 minutes or until bean curd sticks are very soft and broken up.
- Turn off heat and pour egg into soup in a slow steady stream about 10 cm (4 in) above pot while stirring in a single direction to form thin ribbons.
- If serving hot, ladle into individual bowls and serve immediately. If serving cold, leave to cool slightly before refrigerating for at least 1 hour.

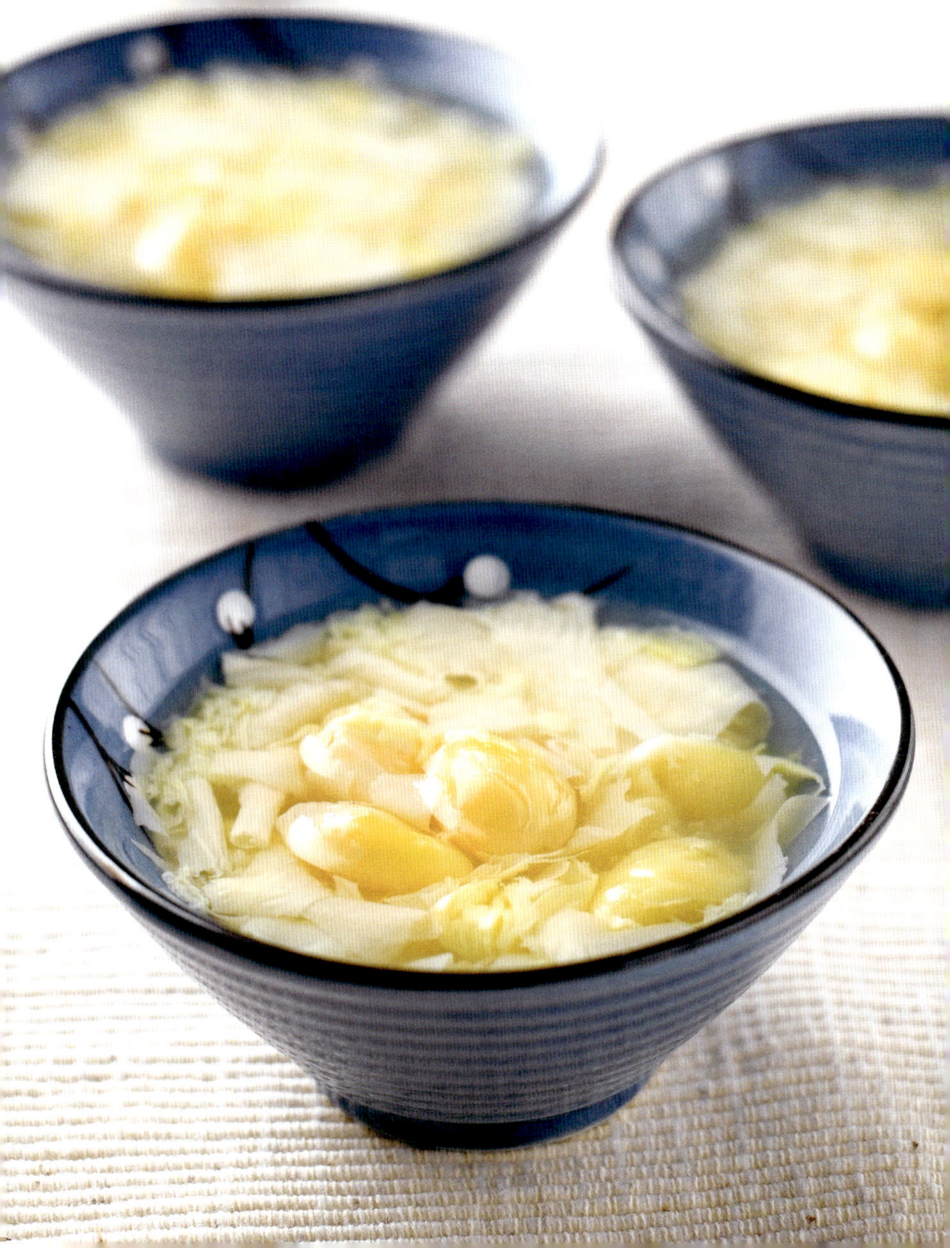

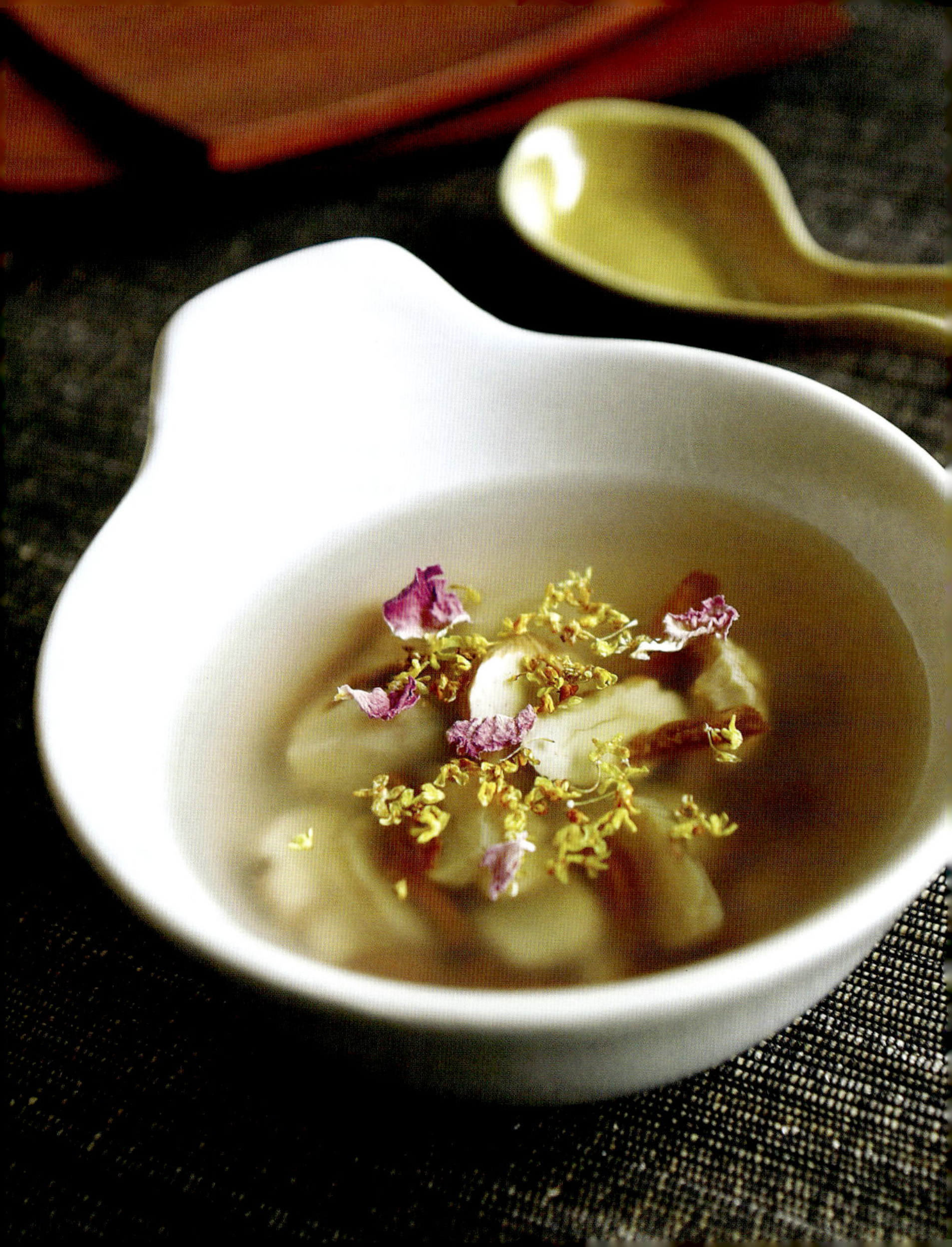

chestnut soup with osmanthus blossoms

Serves 2–3

Osmanthus blossoms, or *gui hua*, add a light floral fragrance to this dessert. Omit if unavailable.

INGREDIENTS

Arrow root powder	2 Tbsp
Chestnuts	110 g (4 oz), peeled and sliced
Sugar	110 g (4 oz)
Candied plums	5, sliced
Sweetened osmanthus blossoms (*gui hua*)	2 tsp
Dried rose petals	3

METHOD

- Add $1/2$ Tbsp water to arrow root powder to form a paste. Adjust the amount of water as necessary.
- Bring 500 ml (16 fl oz / 2 cups) water to the boil in a pot. Add chestnut slices and sugar. Stir in arrow root paste and return to the boil.
- Turn off heat and add sliced plums, sweetened osmanthus blossoms and rose petals.
- Ladle into serving bowls and serve.

barley soup Serves 4

This barley soup is chock-full of ingredients. Serve as a snack between meals, as it may be too heavy for dessert.

INGREDIENTS

Barley	110 g (4 oz)
Dried lily buds	50 g (2 oz), soaked to soften
Gingko nuts	50 g (2 oz), soaked to soften
Lotus seeds	50 g (2 oz), soaked to soften
Water	1.5 litres (48 fl oz / 6 cups)
Dried red dates	50 g (2 oz)
Preserved plums	5
Dried longan pulp	2 Tbsp
Haw candy	10 g ($1/3$ oz)
Sugar	85 g (3 oz)
Rock sugar	85 g (3 oz)
Corn flour (cornstarch)	1 Tbsp, mixed with 2 Tbsp water

METHOD

- Steam barley for 25 minutes. Steam soaked dried lily buds, gingko nuts and lotus seeds for 15 minutes.

- Bring water to the boil in a pot. Add all ingredients except corn flour mixture. Allow water to return to the boil, then lower heat. Remove from heat and stir in corn flour mixture to thicken soup slightly.

- Ladle into serving bowls and serve hot.

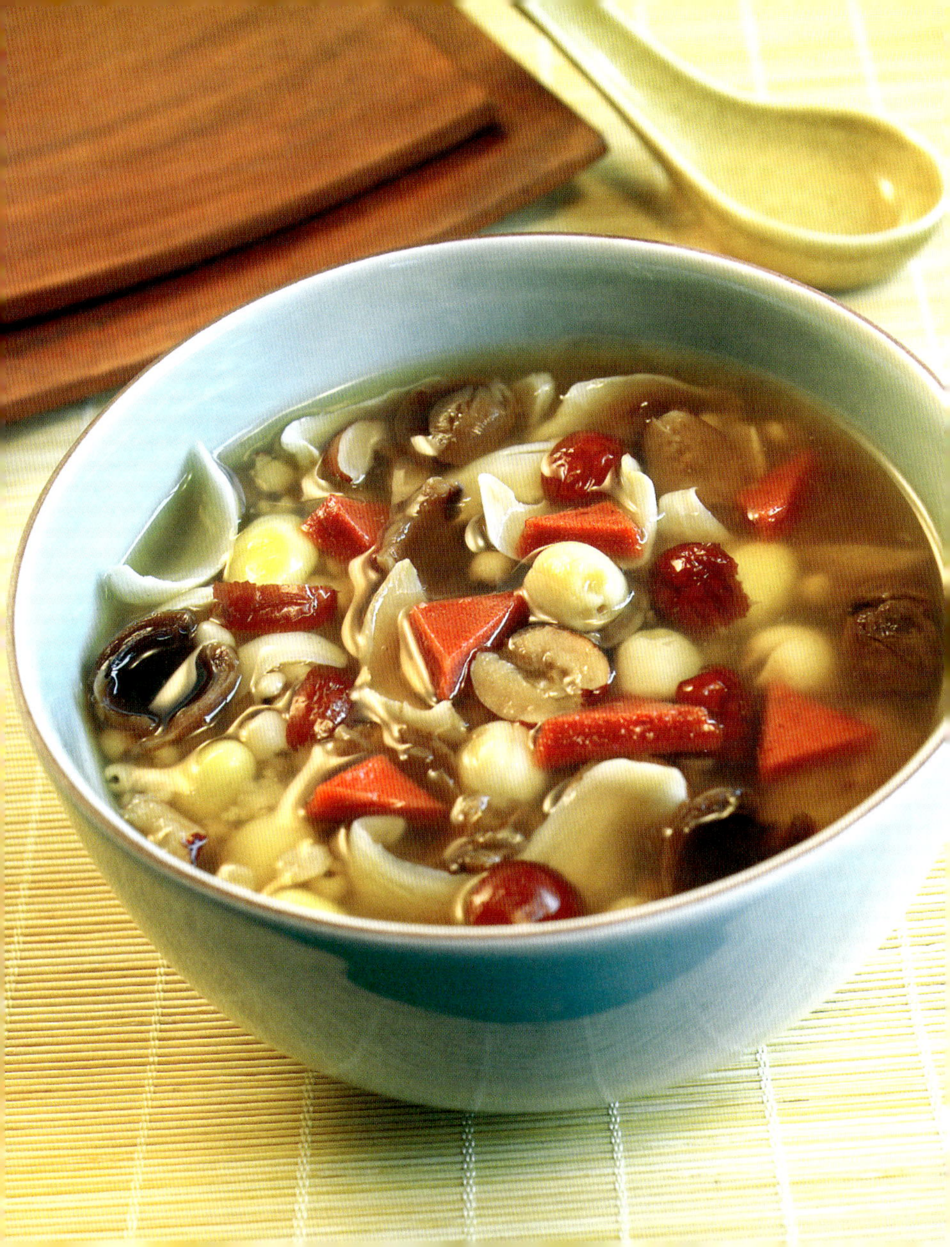

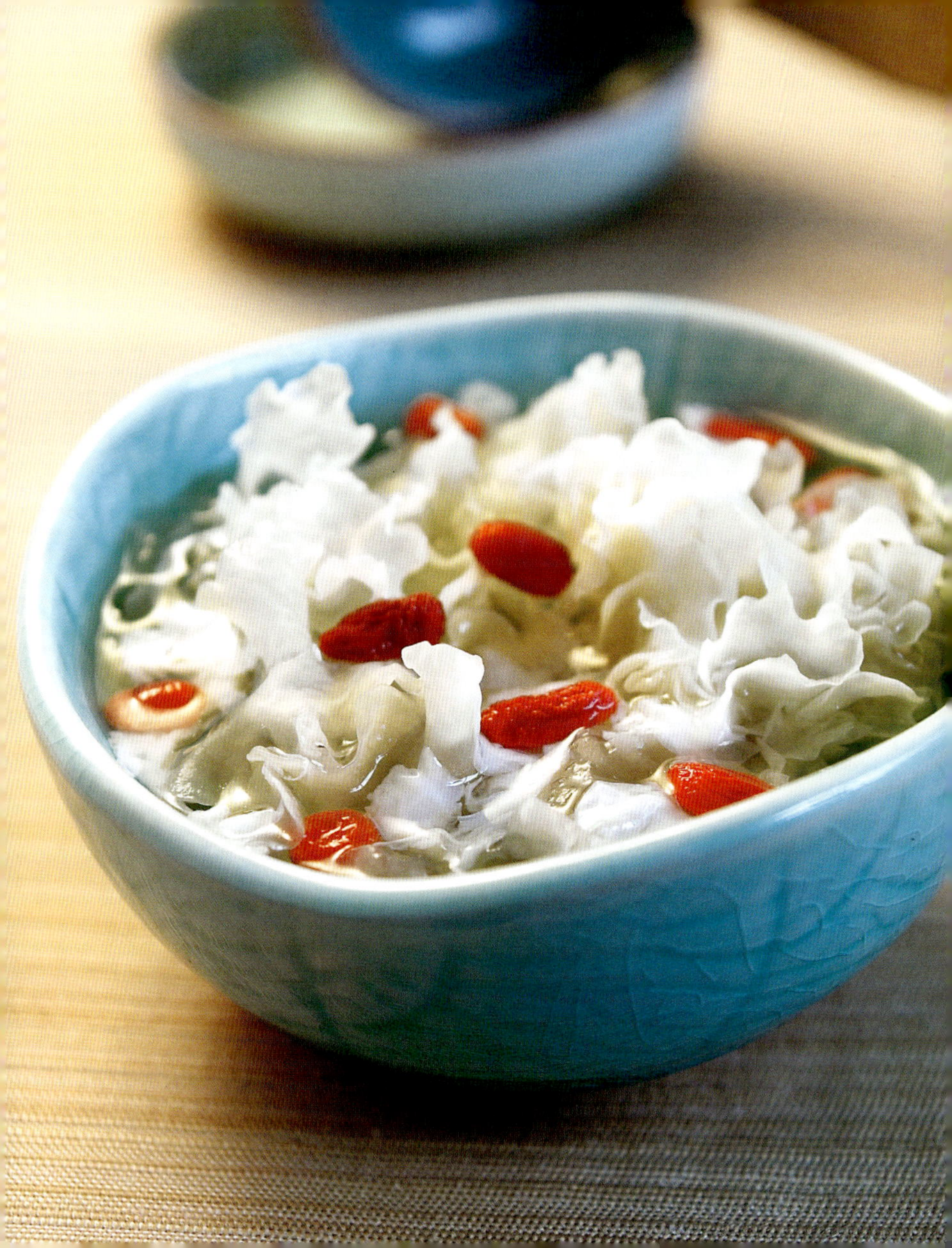

white fungus and wolfberry soup Serves 4

A fitting end to a dim sum meal, this sweet dessert is packed with the crunchy goodness of white fungus and sight-improving Chinese wolfberries.

INGREDIENTS

Water	1 litre (32 fl oz / 4 cups)
Dried white fungus	60 g (2 oz), soaked in warm water for 1 hour until slightly expanded
Rock sugar	110 g (4 oz)
Chinese wolfberries	3 Tbsp
Egg whites	2, lightly beaten

METHOD

- Place water and white fungus into a pot. Bring water to the boil, then lower heat, cover and simmer for 1 hour.
- Add rock sugar and Chinese wolfberries. Cook for 10 minutes, then stir in egg whites. Skim off any foam that appears.
- Ladle into serving bowls and serve hot.

weights and measures

Quantities for this book are given in Metric, Imperial and American (spoon and cup) measures. Standard spoon and cup measurements used are: 1 tsp = 5 ml, 1 Tbsp = 15 ml, 1 cup = 250 ml. All measures are level unless otherwise stated.

Liquid And Volume Measures

Metric	Imperial	American
5 ml	1/6 fl oz	1 teaspoon
10 ml	1/3 fl oz	1 dessertspoon
15 ml	1/2 fl oz	1 tablespoon
60 ml	2 fl oz	1/4 cup (4 tablespoons)
85 ml	2 1/2 fl oz	1/3 cup
90 ml	3 fl oz	3/8 cup (6 tablespoons)
125 ml	4 fl oz	1/2 cup
180 ml	6 fl oz	3/4 cup
250 ml	8 fl oz	1 cup
300 ml	10 fl oz (1/2 pint)	1 1/4 cups
375 ml	12 fl oz	1 1/2 cups
435 ml	14 fl oz	1 3/4 cups
500 ml	16 fl oz	2 cups
625 ml	20 fl oz (1 pint)	2 1/2 cups
750 ml	24 fl oz (1 1/5 pints)	3 cups
1 litre	32 fl oz (1 3/5 pints)	4 cups
1.25 litres	40 fl oz (2 pints)	5 cups
1.5 litres	48 fl oz (2 2/5 pints)	6 cups
2.5 litres	80 fl oz (4 pints)	10 cups

Dry Measures

Metric	Imperial
30 grams	1 ounce
45 grams	1 1/2 ounces
55 grams	2 ounces
70 grams	2 1/2 ounces
85 grams	3 ounces
100 grams	3 1/2 ounces
110 grams	4 ounces
125 grams	4 1/2 ounces
140 grams	5 ounces
280 grams	10 ounces
450 grams	16 ounces (1 pound)
500 grams	1 pound, 1 1/2 ounces
700 grams	1 1/2 pounds
800 grams	1 3/4 pounds
1 kilogram	2 pounds, 3 ounces
1.5 kilograms	3 pounds, 4 1/2 ounces
2 kilograms	4 pounds, 6 ounces

Oven Temperature

	°C	°F	Gas Regulo
Very slow	120	250	1
Slow	150	300	2
Moderately slow	160	325	3
Moderate	180	350	4
Moderately hot	190/200	375/400	5/6
Hot	210/220	410/425	6/7
Very hot	230	450	8
Super hot	250/290	475/550	9/10

Length

Metric	Imperial
0.5 cm	1/4 inch
1 cm	1/2 inch
1.5 cm	3/4 inch
2.5 cm	1 inch

Abbreviation

tsp	teaspoon
Tbsp	tablespoon
g	gram
kg	kilogram
ml	millilitre